THE BOOTLEGGERS OF MONTANA MOUNTAIN

A RURAL NEW JERSEY COMMUNITY'S PROHIBITION EXPERIENCE

By

Richard H. Dalrymple Jr.

Ragged Ridge Press, USA

Copyright © 2017 by Richard H. Dalrymple Jr.
All rights reserved, including the right to reproduce this book or portions thereof in any form whatsoever without permission in writing by the author.

Based on Vintage Book Template by: David Haden.

ISBN-13:9780692856536
ISBN-10:0692856536

Library of Congress Control number:
2017935855
Ragged Ridge Press, Phillipsburg, N.J.

Ragged Ridge Press

Printed in the United States of America.
2017

Cover photo: Several large stills of approximately 500 gallon capacity each which operated in Warren County, New Jersey during Prohibition. The four men, including one who is armed, are clearly proud of the operation. The men are unidentified; however, it is noteworthy that the smiling man standing in front with the gun is wearing a badge...

(Courtesy of the Warren County Historical Society)

Contents

Introduction & Acknowledgements   *i*
Foreword: America's Love of Alcohol and the Age of Prohibition   *v*

One: The Old Man of the Mountain   1
Two: Bob Clower   9
Three: The Kobers, Magnantes, Ghettis, & Westers   14
Four: The Blow-up, The Fohrs, Old Man Williamson, & The Richlines   19
Five: The Smith Brothers: Walt, Harry, & Clarence   23
Six: The Searles Brothers   31
Seven: Clint Hartung & His Neighbors Leo Lommason, & John Pavoni of Roxburg   33
Eight: The Denkers, The Biergarten, & Thorpes Grove of Low's Hollow   36
Nine: The Steeles, The Unangsts, The Apgars, & The Other Smiths   39
Ten: The Belview "Chicken Operation"   46
Eleven: A Local Bootlegger Outlet Surfaces   48
Twelve: Old Times Die Hard: After the Fall   59
Thirteen: Times May Change, But Memories Live On   72

Postscript   *86*

In Memoriam   *89*

Appendix i: Excerpts from Press Articles About Bob Clower 1923-1924   *90*

Appendix ii: Phillipsburg Speakeasies Active During Prohibition   *101*

Appendix iii: Brief Chronology of Events Appearing in the Easton Express/Easton Argus 1920-1933   *104*

Introduction & Acknowledgements

This account began as a serendipitous tangent stemming from my research into the histories of some of the oldest families of Harmony Township, a bucolic farming community that stretches along the Delaware River in Warren County, New Jersey, my home. All was going well in this endeavor until I focused on the Smith family and met Dick Smith, whose fascinating stories abruptly redirected my focus to a momentous epoch in American history: Prohibition. As bootlegging had once been the principle income source for many of families on Montana Mountain where Dick lived, this diversion was thus a natural line of inquiry. It soon, however, became a consuming task, leading me from one fascinating source to another, opening windows to the past. The human mind is a funny thing. An octogenarian or nonagenarian may forget what happened last week, but will vividly recall the events of their youth as if they happened yesterday. Whereas I fondly recall the halcyon Norman Rockwell days when fresh milk and bread were delivered to your door (and freezing milk erupted from bottles on winter doorsteps), when mail was delivered with a smile and chat, those minds are rich with vivid memories of a more distant past, when horse drawn wagons plied the roads with early motor vehicles and when bootleggers and rum runners were in their heyday. I was privileged to have had those fascinating windows opened to me through the eyes of some who had been there to bear witness as America learned hard lessons which paved the way to what it is today. Stories seemed to jump at me wherever I turned, riveting stories of those eventful, tumultuous times either first-hand or through vivid family tales—stories that needed to be harvested for posterity... tales that needed to live on. I only hope that others will now enjoy reading these stories as much as I did when I first heard them from the friends and family of the actors involved, people I have come to respect and admire.

It is worth noting that 2020 will mark the 100th anniversary of the enactment of Prohibition and it will not be long before any first hand witnesses to life during that momentous period will be gone. I cannot therefore proceed without first acknowledging my deep gratitude to my good friend, Dick Smith, who always warmly welcomed me into his home to listen with rapture to his personal account of the life and times of the colorful characters of that age in our community. I am also indebted to others who shared with me their memories of the activities of their friends and relatives during those bygone days including Joe "Red" Smith and his daughter Joanne, Alan and Joan Apgar and their daughter Cindy, Doris McKeever, Harry L. and Donald Smith, and their sister Arlene (Smith) Andrews, Barry, Sherry and Mark "Skip" Smith, Rose (Smith) Kinney, Dale Hamlen, Claude Rudd, Ralph and Ray Raub, Lois (Tillman) Walsh, Bruce Unangst, Harold Vannatta, Wayne Deremer, Andy Thorp, Mary (Weighurst) Warden, George DeVault, Dawn Piazza, Terry and Nelson Lee, Jake Bungert, Barry Miller, Nancy (Miller) Schnoover, Vivian (Miller) Stecker, Caroline and Dick Denker, Bill Grainer, Les Kober, John Stasyshyn, Carl "Corky" Richline, Richard Ducklow, Clair Krepps, Maryann Ignatz, Bob Hamlen, Bill Shepherd, Skip Meglic, Tom Vincent, George McBride, Roger Whippen, John Fulmer, Cliff Oberly, and the staff of the Warren County Historical Society. I am also most grateful to Dr. Richard F. Hope, the staff of the Lehigh University Linderman Library, James Deegan and Kaitlin Martin of the Easton Express-Times, and Elaine Billiard, William Lear, and Sharon Gothard of the Easton, Pennsylvania Public Library for their help in my research. My wife, Karma, has also been a constant support, assisting me to recover relevant press articles not only during the Prohibition period (1920-33), but during the twenty years thereafter. Love is patient. Love is kind. I'm a lucky man. My three children have been equally supportive and have assisted me in proof-reading.

During this work, I have also had the pleasure of meeting a modern day bootlegger, known as "Sneaky Pete" who diligently and faithfully carries on the time honored tradition of home distilling, following the same methods used by the individuals described herein and I would like to thank him for educating me on these processes. The tradition thus lives on...

I would also like to point out that although the families described herein may have been involved in activities that became illegal during Prohibition, they also contained patriots who fought and sacrificed their lives in uniform for the freedom and liberty that all Americans cherish and which they strongly felt were being violated by the 18th Amendment to the Constitution. In rebelling against what they considered an unjust law, they were thus only echoing the immortal words inscribed on one of the banners our revolutionary ancestors marched under: "Don't Tread on Me!"

This book is dedicated to my dear friend, Dick Smith of Montana Mountain, who celebrated his 97th birthday on February 1st 2016.

Foreword

AMERICA'S LOVE OF ALCOHOL AND THE AGE OF PROHIBITION

Although temperance groups in the US had been advocating abstinence from alcohol since the 1830s, alcoholic beverages were very much a part of American life since before the Revolution. The Mayflower's hold was in fact filled with barrels of beer and in colonial New England, bells habitually rang twice a day for "grog time."

The Whiskey Rebellion which erupted after Congress passed a bill in 1791 introduced by Secretary of Treasury Alexander Hamilton for a federal excise tax of between six and nine cents per gallon on whiskey to help pay off the Revolutionary War debt became a defining event in American history when George Washington himself led a militia force of 13,000 men to quash the rebellion in 1794. In doing so, however, Washington's actions were fiscal and not moral, as he ran a distillery of his own at Mt. Vernon. During the war Washington had even written to the Continental Congress proposing the erection of public distilleries stating that "the benefits arising from moderate use of strong liquor have been experienced in all armies and are not to be disputed".[1] Nevertheless, when Thomas Jefferson abolished this hated excise tax in 1801, he made himself an immortal hero to the mountain folk and whiskey production once again flourished. It is worth noting that many

---

[1] *The Writings of George Washington.* Letter to the President of Congress. Nesamini Camp August 16th 1777. Ironically, Albert Gallatin, a resident of Western Pennsylvania and one of the insurrectionists during the Whiskey Rebellion, later became Secretary of Treasury under Jefferson and Madison.

cash poor country folk in remote areas who depended on crops such as corn, barley, or apples/cider for a living would distill much of their production. This was done not only because the conversion of such produce into spirits facilitated transport and eliminated spoilage and waste but also because the alcohol was treated as cash in the marketplace. A gallon of whiskey at that time would fetch 50 cents which had a lot more buying power than today.

Applejack played an important part in the early history of Warren County, New Jersey. It is said for example that before the Revolution the residents of a village once known as "Crow Valley," being unhappy with its name, met in the tavern owned by Samuel Hackett and agreed that it be named after the man who would donate the most apple brandy. Hackett, desirous of fame, then announced that he would donate a hogshead of good Jersey applejack (63+ gallons). No one could match him, and the village's name became Hackettstown.[2] During the 1850s Warren County had seven operational distilleries of which two were located in Lower Harmony Township: one operated by David Howell and another operated by Tindale, Drinkhouse and Vreman.[3] A map of 1852 also indicates an "Apple Distillery" on Montana Mountain owned by D. Beer at the source of Lopatcong Creek which runs from Upper to Lower Harmony. It is likely that all three distilleries were located along this water source (the nearby Merrill Creek most likely also had some) since cold mountain water from such creeks is essential for distillery operations. During the 19th century the creek also supplied water for three Grist Mills owned by Moses Allen, John

---

2 See *The History of Applejack or Apple Brandy in New Jersey from Colonial Times to the Present*. Harry B. Weiss, New Jersey Agricultural Society, Trenton 1975. p247-248 (quoting the Proceedings of the NJ Historical Society (70 (1):56-60. 1952). In neighboring Hunterdon County, Jugtown mountain traces its name to the jugs that moonshiners would hide on rock ledges there to avoid detection by Prohibition gents. (Source: *Hunterdon County Division of Parks and Recreation*).

3 Kirkbrides *New Jersey Business Directory for 1850 and 1851* and *The History of Applejack or Apple Brandy in New Jersey from Colonial Times to the Present*" Harry B. Weiss New Jersey Agricultural Society, Trenton, 1975. p248-249. By 1860 New Jersey had a total of 52 distilleries producing 1.5 million gallons of whiskey, high wines and alcohol. (ref: *Preliminary Report: The Eight Census 1860*; Jos. C.G. Kennedy, Washington: Government Printing Office p178).

Holden, and William Vannatta.[4] In 1852, the township had a population of 1,561 living in 286 dwellings and had 120 farms.[5]

The area is rich in history having once been partly owned by Daniel Martin to whom George II granted the exclusive privilege of operating a ferry over the Delaware at the mouth of the Lopatcong Creek in 1739. Martin also served as Sheriff of Hunterdon County, was (along with Benjamin Franklin) one of the first members of the American Philosophical Society, and became the first rector of a youth academy which later became known as the University of Pennsylvania.[6] Once known as Scott's Mountain, its inhabitants were well known for their firm Tory orientation during the American Revolution. Some of the prominent family names there were Rush, Prall, and Insley. Jacob Rush's neighbor was a man named John Blair whose grandson, John Insley Blair, became one of the wealthiest men in the world, being president of 16 railroad companies and having amassed an estate worth about $45 billion in today's dollars at the time of his death.[7]

Although moderation and restraint were preached early on, by 1869 groups like the National Prohibition Party, formed that year, advocated the total prohibition of alcohol, blaming it for many crimes including debauchery and murder. Excise taxes on alcohol had however, helped finance the Civil War and were a main source of government revenue.[8] That changed when income taxes were introduced in 1913 with the

---

4 Some mills had a duel purpose. Amazingly an Account Book belonging to Moses Allen with the heading "For Stilling" surfaced in North Carolina and has found its way home to Harmony, N.J. Its first entry dated March 10th 1803 lists the cost of "Materials for setting up Stills" which were obtained in Philadelphia. The cost for two stills included $378.55 for stills/boilers & apparatus, $110 for patents, $61.50 for 41 mashing hogsheads in addition to travel, copper, blacksmith/miscellaneous costs totaling $582.85. The listings of Allen's clients reads like a Who's Who of the community, including names like Amey, Beers, Miller, Cline, Rush, Smith, Hoff, DeWitt, Steel, Vannatta, Davison, Young, Shoemaker and Dalrymple among others. (The current owner of this ledger book wishes to remain anonymous).
5 *Map of Warren County NJ*, by D. Mc Carty 1852.
6 Ref: *Easton Express* article "David Martin Not a Mere Ferryman" of April 25th 1938 p.8.
7 See http://www.investors.com/news/management/leaders-and-success/john-blair-made-fortune-in-railroads. *The Phillipsburg Star* reported in an article of February 24th 1934 entitled "Believe it or Not" that once after eating in a railroad restaurant in a small Western town, the cashier, seeing his shabby clothes, asked Blair if he belonged to the railroad. His response was "No my dear young lady..The railroad belongs to me!"
8 Interestingly, a drink consisting of four ounces of applejack and eight ounces of hard cider was later known in northern New Jersey as a "Stonewall Jackson" after the Civil War general. It was said that on drinking it, the drinker wouldn't know if he were in Sussex, England or Sussex, New Jersey! Ref: *The History of Applejack or Apple Brandy in New Jersey from Colonial Times to the Present*" Harry B. Weiss New Jersey Agricultural Society, Trenton, 1975 p89

passage of the 16th Amendment, thus giving strength to temperance groups such as the Woman's Christian Temperance Union, founded in 1873, and the Anti Saloon League, formed on 1893. Jack London, a heavy drinker and famous author of The Call of the Wild, also became a catalyst and poster child for the prohibition movement with the publication of his semi-autobiographical novel, John Barleycorn in 1913, which highlighted the self destructive evils of alcohol. In doing so he was only strengthening the case already made in a shocking earlier book published in 1854 entitled, *Ten Nights in a Bar-Room and What I Saw There* by T.S. Arthur which became the second most popular book of the Victorian Age after Harriet Beecher Stowe's *Uncle Tom's Cabin*.

By 1916, over half of the states in the US had statutes prohibiting alcohol. One was Maine, where itinerant liquor sellers selling swigs of whiskey from bottles strapped beneath their pant legs became known as "bootleggers." In the midst of World War I the scales tipped even more when on December 18th, 1917 Congress passed the 18th Amendment which banned the manufacture, transportation and sale of intoxicating liquors and passed it to the States for ratification. In the meantime, on November 21st 1918, to save grain for the war effort, President Wilson signed the Wartime Prohibition Act temporarily banning the sale of alcoholic beverages having an alcohol content of greater than 2.75% (although ironically the Armistice had already been signed on November 11th). Two months later, on January 16th 1919, the provisions of the 18th Amendment which banned "the manufacture, sale, or transportation of intoxicating liquors" were ratified and set to become the law of the land one year later.

The Volstead Act of October 1919, which Congress passed on October 28th 1919 over President Wilson's veto, subsequently clarified the law by defining intoxicating liquors as "beer, wine, or other intoxicating malt or vinous liquors... which contain one-half of 1 per centum or more of alcohol by volume" and established specific fines and jail sentences for violations. Thus began a tumultuous period of nearly fourteen years that lasted until December 5th 1933, known as "the Noble Experiment",[9] which left an indelible mark on American history and produced some notoriously unforgettable characters.

---

9 Note: Although the term "Noble Experiment" is attributed to Herbert Hoover, he didn't directly use this precise term. It arose from the text of his letter of 23 February 1928 written to Senator Wm. Borah which read "Our country has deliberately undertaken a great social and economic experiment, noble in motive and far reaching in purpose."

The original provisions of the law, however, did not ban the actual drinking of liquor and since Prohibition took effect a full year after the Amendment's ratification, individuals and private clubs bought and stockpiled huge volumes of alcohol before the law took effect.[10] As the Volstead Act also allowed alcohol consumption if prescribed by a doctor, medical prescriptions ran rampant although some of these "patients" were in fact already dead and buried.[11] Those who did not stockpile their booze in advance or know a "good" doctor could still obtain alcohol through the underground, either via the mob network of illegal contraband from Canadian or Caribbean rum-runners, or from the stills of local bootleggers who seized the opportunity to make their fortune despite the risks. The operations of risk-takers and gangsters including secret bars (speakeasies or blind pigs) were facilitated by underpaid under-qualified and/or corrupt government officials who preferred bribes/payoffs to the dangerous enforcement of laws they didn't really believe in. Those unwilling to take risks had a choice: "America, Love it or Leave it" and some, having fled the ravages of WWI in Europe for the Land of Liberty, simply decided to go home.[12]

New Jersey's anti-Prohibition Democratic Governor Edward I. Edwards, elected in 1919, in what was called "The Applejack Campaign," vowed that his state would remain "as wet as the Atlantic Ocean". However, with Nebraska's ratification on January 16th of that year, the two-thirds majority was reached and the new Federal law was set to take effect one year later, on January 16th, 1920, the same year that women obtained the right to vote. Despite New Jersey's foot dragging, by March 9th 1922, it reluctantly became the 46th and last of the 48 states to ratify the amendment (two states: Connecticut and Rhode Island, rejected it) and the Feds made it clear that they would enforce the law.[13] Many states and municipalities however, remained uncoop-

---

10 Thus, the Yale Club in New York City was able to stock up enough liquor to see the club through the repeal of Prohibition in 1933 and the mother of film star Mary Pickford bought out the entire inventory of a liquor store in Los Angeles to cover her needs.
11 The authority of doctors to prescribe alcohol for medicinal purposes was later limited by the Willis-Campbell Act of 1921.
12 An article "Prohibition Driving Foreign Born Citizens From America" of 12 March 1920 p1 in The Easton Express/ Easton Argus reported that during the first two months of the year there were 44,000 arrivals through Ellis Island compared with 49,000 departures.
13 By this time however, New Jersey's dry legislators had already passed over Governor Edward's veto its dry law (The Van Ness Act) which took effect from midnight April 31st 1921. This act was later ruled unconstitutional as it allowed imprisonment without the right of a trial by jury and was replaced in March 1922 by the Hobart Act which required trial by jury.

erative and citizens felt, like Robin Hood, that since government had no business legislating morality they should feel no guilt or shame in breaking any such law...in fact they took pride in it! Opportunities also now abounded for supplying an illicit demand and those willing to take the risk would be rewarded with enormous returns for doing so. In a term coined in January 1924 following a contest with 25,000 entries aimed "to stab awake the lawless drinker," anyone who ignored the edict and either bought, sold, or drank liquor illegally became known as a "Scofflaw". The prosecution of such violations soon flooded the courts. In New Jersey, over 90 percent of the criminal cases filed in its Federal courts during the fiscal year ending 30 June 1925 involved liquor law violations: of 2,388 cases initiated, 2,124 involved liquor; of 1,131 convictions, 1011 were liquor related. Of the $301,000 in fines collected, $284,000 was from liquor cases. Such numbers were unprecedented.[14] Some New Jersey towns actually offered rewards to anyone providing conclusive evidence of the selling of intoxicating liquors leading to a conviction. Washington Borough in Warren County, for example, offered a $50 reward for such information.[15]

New Jersey's Dry Law, the Van Ness Act, introduced in early 1921 by Jennie C. Van Ness (R, Essex), one of the first two women to serve in the State Legislature, passed and became law over the veto of Governor Edwards. The law allowed for severe penalties on the sale and manufacture of alcoholic beverages and for trials before a magistrate without jury. Amazingly, there was no uproar when it took effect after midnight on Saturday, April 31st, 1921. Local Press for Warren County New Jersey reported the following Monday that there was "no change was noticeable in habits", and that "Those who wanted a bracer went to the same old haunts and got it at the same old price."[16] Life was, however, about to change.[17] The first case in Warren County involving enforcement of the Van Ness law took place on July 8th, 1921 and involved a saloon keeper who was fined $75 plus court costs by a

---

14 *Easton Express* article "Booze Cases Flood Courts" of August 19th 1925 p8.
15 Ibid. article "Would Stop Booze Selling" of 5 November 1920 p8.
16 Ibid. article "New Dry Law is Effective" of May 2nd 1921 p8.
17 It had in fact already changed at a cost. After the passage of the Federal law the previous year, traditional sources of alcohol were drying up and illicit outlets sprouted up. On April 2nd 1920 the *Easton Express* reported in an article entitled "Farmer Drank Beer and Died" (p10) that Emanuel Creagar, a mail carrier from Roxburg, went blind after drinking two glasses of draft beer at a farm sale and later died from wood alcohol poisoning. Such incidents were not uncommon.

judge without the benefit of a jury of his peers.[18]

In the fall of 1926, a tough teetotaling Army colonel named Ira Reeves took charge of the federal government's New Jersey district Prohibition headquarters in Newark. Reeves saw himself as a "Prohibition St. Patrick" to chase the snakes of demon rum out of New Jersey and went to work with a vengeance, raiding several booze plants a day. In less than a year, he saw it was a losing battle saying – "Keep Jersey sober? Might as well ask Jersey drivers to obey the speed limit!" He later wrote, "There were just as many bootleggers, making bigger profits than before," and "There were doubtless just as many wildcat stills, cutting plants, breweries, ale plants, roadhouses, saloons and speakeasies as before my ambitious crusade." Idle factories were put to use as illegal distilleries. At the rail yards, cargo holds labeled "Jersey tomatoes" or "produce" were really carrying something totally different.

William Walter, Trenton's police chief, whose best friend was Victor Cooper, the local "beer baron", gave his personal protection to bootleggers and threatened to arrest any dry agent who came to town to disturb things. Trenton was a melting pot of Italians, Irish, Germans and Poles, as was Newark. These groups cherished their Old World traditions, which included a lot of social drinking and they were not about to change. Thus, despite its concerted effort to control alcohol possession, distribution, and use, the government failed dismally. One national survey covering every state in the Union revealed that arrests for drunkenness increased in 457 representative places from 250,000 in 1920 to 650,000 in 1924. Arrests for drunkenness increased 484 percent in New York, 1062 percent in D.C. and 578 percent in Scranton between 1916 and 1924[19]; moreover, as is well known, mob activities thrived. Nationwide, during the first nine months of 1923 alone, 2,000 lives were lost from poison booze alone (90 percent of bootleg booze was estimated to be poisonous) with many more attributed to alcohol related motor accidents.[20]

In 1926, drunk driving was the most frequent offence reported to

---

18 *Easton Express* article "Fined under Vanness Law" of July 9th 1921 p8. The month before, the postmaster of Milford NJ, in a gesture of support for the new law poured at the request of his mother, a bottle of whiskey manufactured by John Duckworth at Green's Bridge, Phillipsburg NJ in May 1820 into a canal race!! Ref Easton Express article *"Century Old Whisky Dumped into Race"* of 11 June 1921.
19 *Easton Express* article "Drunkenness Prevails in US Like Never Before" 13 April 1926 p.1.
20 Ibid. article "Nationwide Survey Shows that 90 percent of Bootleg Liquor is Poisonous to Greater of Less Degree" of 4 October 1923

the New Jersey Motor Vehicle Commission, resulting in 1,200 driver's license revocations.[21] There was also the toll on human life. During the first four years of Prohibition, 37 Federal Agents were killed along with more than 40 bootleggers and over $50 million had been spent on law enforcement.[22] The Roaring Twenties came and went and gradually the tide began to turn against the Temperance Movement and Prohibition. Especially after the Stock Market crash of October 1929 followed by the start of Great Depression people needed the jobs and the government needed the money that the repeal of Prohibition would bring through excise taxes. Finally, on December 5th, 1933, the 21st Amendment to the U.S. Constitution which repealed the 18th Amendment was ratified and alcohol once again became legal. The "Noble Experiment" had run its course and while hard lessons had been learned, legendary figures have become a permanent part of American folklore…

Ira Reeves later reminisced about his frustrations as the Prohibition enforcement chief for New Jersey. Local Police departments not only dragged their feet, but openly obstructed his work. He never forgot dispatching three of his officers on the night of January 20th, 1927 to check out a report of a beer warehouse at Market and Broad streets in Trenton. The dry agents had no sooner appeared when a mob of angry citizens surrounded them outside the warehouse and threatened to beat them up. When one agent fired into the air to disperse the crowd, a nearby patrol cop was alerted. The cop's reaction was immediate: to arrest the federal agents for carrying guns without licenses![23]

The rural folk on Montana Mountain in Harmony Township, Warren County, New Jersey with a population of 1,311 in 1931 (250 less than in 1852)[24], mostly eking a living from agricultural activities, did not simply stand by while the ill conceived "Noble Experiment" ran its course. Like many who objected to it, they rebelled, taking full advantage of the opportunity to "make hay while the sun was shining." Such rural mountain communities are tight-knit with close marital bonds and these families looked out for each other. It is thus not surprising that when the Federal agents planned raids on the mountains during the Prohibition period, they were often not successful. Having Levi

---

21 *The Washington Star* newspaper article "Drunken Drivers Lead" of 7 January 1926 p1 Sect 3.
22 Ibid, article "Prohibition Fatalities" of 30 October 1924 p8 Sect 1.
23 For references to Reeves see www.capitalcentury.com/1926.html and article: 1926: Wet and Wild Prohibition Days by Jon Blackwell.
24 Source: booklet *Warren County New Jersey- 1931* issued by the Warren Co. NJ Board of Chosen Freeholders.

Mackey, the brother of Civil War Veteran William Mackey of Harmony, as Sheriff of Warren County from 1926 to 1929, at the height of Prohibition, may have helped. In fact, I heard from some local sources that, in this capacity, Levi took special care to look after his neighbors and friends during this tumultuous time. When he got word that a Federal raid was being planned, he reputedly would drive around the mountain to sound the alarm: "The Feds are coming!" During an interview years later, he reminisced that back then "there was beer brewing in every cellar and liquor stills in every woodlot."[25]

---

25 Ref: Mackey's obituary published in *The Star*, Washington N.J. of 26 January 1961 p13.

Chapter One

THE OLD MAN OF THE MOUNTAIN

On February 1st, 2014 Richard "Dick" Smith, who lives on Pleasant Hollow Road off the Harmony Brass Castle Road in Harmony Township New Jersey, turned ninety-five years of age. One would never guess by looking at him that he was born in 1919 since he was spryer than someone twenty years younger and had a memory that left you in awe. As he was well known to the local old-timers and reputably knew a great deal about the local history of Montana Mountain where he lived, he was thus recommended to me and I thus sought him out.

As I knocked at his door, I saw through the window a man sitting at his kitchen table with a newspaper spread before him, totally engrossed. He rose and warmly welcomed me in. Sitting at his table, talk of the old times on the mountain came easy. Dick, in fact, claimed to be the oldest man on the mountain and an authority on its early notoriety for a favorite economic pastime: bootlegging. Memories of the distant past remained fresh in his mind despite the years elapsed—especially those of the tumultuous times during Prohibition and the Second World War. Such reminiscing brought many of the prominent local actors back to life. One of the first things Dick did when he noticed my interest was to show me his prized 5 gallon still, which he proudly told me he had bought for 35 cents.

During our conversation, my curiosity turned to a picture of a busty woman taped to the window above his kitchen table. His response was, "you know it's a curious thing, I can go anywhere in this kitchen and her eyes follow me! She watches over me!"

Although the Smiths were well known as prominent moonshiners on the mountain, Dick Smith's family was not connected to any of the old Smith lines of the township. His father, Rufus, and Irish born mother, Mary Walker, had only arrived on Montana Mountain in 1918 from Bushkill, Pennsylvania settling on the 66 acre Sheep Rock Farm on Montana Road which included an 8 acre apple orchard.[1] Dick was born there on April 1st the following year, one of five boys and a girl. The farm was just down the road from the old stone Smith Quaker meetinghouse in Harmony, but lay partially in neighboring Franklin Township. Dick remembers as a young boy his family being called "outsiders" and "damned Yankees". It soon became clear why: the neighbors all around him were rebels involved in the highly profitable but also, from 1920, highly illegal bootleg whiskey business and the arrival of any newcomers on their turf was viewed suspiciously as a potential threat or possible competition. The family thus initially traversed tough times. Dick remembers one year when his father paid his property taxes by trapping skunks for which he received $3-$4 per hide. After learning that his neighbors were making illegal applejack and realizing that he would risk their collective ire if he started his own operation, Rufus made a wise decision and did the next best thing: he began selling them the cider from his apples, which earned him $10 per 50 gallon barrel (good money in those days!). Dick still fondly remembers as a child sitting in the back of a horse drawn wagon loaded with apples driven by his father down the hill to the Smith Cider Press in nearby Lows Hollow and later returning back up the hill with full barrels of cider to a ready market. As a cider supplier, Rufus's neighbors quickly became steadfast friends and the family's situation notably improved. These were heady days and the cider market was insatiable.

Although his family lived in Harmony Township, Dick remembers attending the nearby grade school in New Village (Franklin Township) as a kid because it was much closer. Old Elijah "Liege" Woolf had the student transport contract for the school for which he received a dollar a day. This transport was by horse and wagon, but Liege would take a short-cut through Rufus's wheat fields on the way, damaging the crops. Rufus cut Liege off by fencing his field thus forcing him to use the road across from the Woolf farm. When Rufus later underbid Liege

---

[1] Dick told me the farm got its name "Sheep Rock" from a previous owner who lost his flock of sheep during a snow blizzard. He later found them alive between large sheets of rock protruding from the ground which provided them natural protection, and he kept them there until Spring. According to a local press article I later found this "legend" involved a farmer named Levi Apgar and occurred between 1856 and 1874. Ref *The Phillipsburger*, article "Montana, Perched On Scott's Mount, Noted for Profusion Of Churches, Severity of Weather" of 17 March 1979.

and got the student transport contract, relations soured even more. In fact, old Liege was so mad that he took his kids out of the New Village School and sent them to the Montana School in Harmony Township which was farther away and probably cost him more.

Dick loved school, but after his father Rufus died suddenly in 1934, he had to quit his 8th grade studies to support the family by running the farm and taking whatever work he could find to support his family. He was hoping to keep the farm, but at age 15 he was under-age and the case had to go to orphan's court which made the decision to sell it and to split the proceeds. The property was thus sold with his mother receiving one-third of the proceeds and the balance being divided amongst the six children: Henry, Leo, Richard, Kathleen, Thomas and John. After the lawyers were paid, Dick remembers his share being only $26. Although he had left school, the Principal, Mr. Seals, had not forgotten his promising student and came to see him to suggest that he go to Washington, NJ to take a test for his grammar school diploma, which he did and proudly passed. Then, remembering his father's words: "you won't amount to a G' damn; all you want to do is hunt and fish," he set out to make his way in the world.

As a "working man" at 15 years of age, Dick would hang around with an older crowd, his co-workers. He would thus often end up in bars after work and remembers with a chuckle getting caught at "The Antlers" in nearby Broadway by the bartender who shouted "Hey you! You're not 21, get out of here!" By age 17, he was making trips out to Chicago driving back Diamond T trucks for a local dealer. He would drive day and night bringing back two trucks per trip, driving one and towing the other, earning $25 per trip. When he got home neighbors who had never travelled would ask him, "What's it like way out there?"

Dick's first "official" job was at the Edison Cement Plant on the Broadway-Asbury Road where, at age 18, he worked in the Power Department. He remembers seeing Thomas Edison himself come to the plant several times while he worked there. Edison would always come by train to the plant, wearing his trademark white duster jacket. After overseeing the plant operations, he would then always go up the mountain behind the plant, known then by what can now only be referred to now obliquely as "The N-word Hill" to look down at the plant to think out his expansion plans and decide what he was going to do next. Many of the approximately 300 plant workers, mostly blacks and immigrants, had built their shacks on the other (Asbury) side of the mountain ridge. After work, big fights and occasional killings occurred there.² Before the war, Dick also worked for some time at the forge at Ingersoll Rand in nearby Phillipsburg.

The Edison Cement Works, New Village, NJ circa 1930 (private collection).

Dick got married in 1942, but his wife Pauline née Petrolati of New Village died tragically in childbirth in early August of that same year attended by a prominent local physician, Doctor Harry B. Bossard, who some now refer to in jest as "Doc Buzzard." To this day, Dick holds this doctor personally responsible for his wife's death since he delayed calling a specialist from Easton despite an obstruction during childbirth. When the specialist was finally called, he asked the doctor and Dick why he had not been called sooner. Had he been called, he said, he could have saved her, but it was now too late; both mother and child died hours later. Pauline was only 27 years old. Dick was heartbroken, despondent, and upset. To add insult to injury, a while later Dick, by chance, came across Bossard on the street in nearby Phillipsburg and the doctor, seeing him, came up to him to remind him that

---

2 Note: In part because of the effect of liquor on labor productivity, both Edison and his close friend and former employee Henry Ford, who visited his New Village plant in July 1931, were strong supporters of Prohibition. On February 15th 1924 in an article, "Find Enough Rum In New Village To Float A Battleship", the *Easton Express/Easton Argus* reported that "Prosecutor Smith has received many complaints from the Edison Portland Cement Company regarding the failure of the employees of the plant..to attend their work regularly" and that he declared that "He saw more booze in the homes of New Village..than he had ever seen in modern wholesale liquor stores in pre-Prohibition days."

the bill for his services was still outstanding. That struck a nerve. Dick's reflexive reply was "Go to hell!" This reaction worked sharply to Dick's disadvantage since Doctor Bossard also sat on the local Draft Board appointed by the Governor's office. The next time Dick saw the doctor was thus at this board when his status was reviewed and abruptly changed from 4A to 1A—the highest draft category: "available for immediate service," after which he was sent off to Newark post haste. That was the memorable day that, in Dick's words, "He fixed my ass!" Doc Bossard never got paid for his service...

Thus, in 1942, at age 23, Dick was enlisted in the US Army, where he served with the 102nd Ozark Infantry Division for 4 and a half years until 1946. Dick was and still is a phenomenal marksman. He told me it was not something he learned, it was simply instinct: "Some people have it and some don't". The Army soon discovered his skill after he easily won a $1 prize offered to anyone who could get a perfect shooting score. The distinction was bittersweet; however, as he was subsequently assigned as a marksman trainer. Money and furloughs were most important to enlisted men. Dick preferred the money, remembering once selling his top place on the furlough list to another soldier in his unit for fifty dollars.

Although Dick never saw active combat during WWII, he is quick to tell you, "That doesn't mean you're out of danger!" In his case, he was, in fact, severely injured during training maneuvers in Louisiana when the live artillery being used fell short, overturning the truck he was in, leaving him with a fractured skull, torn shoulder, and fractured ribs. Later, at Fort Dix, NJ he was unable to pass the physical for war duty due to these injuries and was instead placed in charge of a barracks caring for men returning from the war with battle injuries.

Dick's kid brother Leo, born in 1929, also served his country in the Air Force during the Korean War. Leo later married Gloria Willever and later became known for establishing the successful local Leo B. Smith Insurance Agency. Leo passed away in 2011.

After the war, Dick met Lottie Javitt of Stroudsburg at a popular local hangout: The Rancho near Belvidere. Lottie and her friend needed a ride home and Dick had a car and offered to assist them which eventually led to marriage in 1946. Dick then returned to the forge at Ingersoll Rand where he worked as a millwright with a Harmony neighbor, Chris Denker, until 1955 but had to abruptly quit after being diagnosed with black-lung obtained from breathing metal dust and fumes.

He bought his residential property along the Lopatcong Creek in 1949 from Gordon Rowe through the realtor Paul Cool for $1,750. It consisted of 4.5 acres and a shack. Earl Garris, a contractor from Washington, NJ helped him convert the shack into a comfortable home and in the process taught Dick carpentry. Lottie would not move in, however, until the house had indoor plumbing. Old man Sylvester Hawk of Hutchison, who Dick knew from when they were once neighbors, showed him where to dig for water using a divining rod. Hawk knew his stuff: after digging 24 feet down they hit water and soon an artesian well was operational. With this, Lottie's dream came true and the couple was the first in the neighborhood to have indoor plumbing and a bathroom. This resulted in some jealousy amongst the neighbors, but domestic tranquility in which to raise their two sons Tom and Richard.

With the skills learned from Garris, Dick began his own building contracting business, but it unfortunately didn't last long. After a strike at Ingersoll Rand, he had to lay off his men since the unemployed Ingersoll workers would work for only $1 an hour, much below his rates. He later began work with Westinghouse and GE installing turbines. Among other projects, he was proud to have worked at Yards Creek near Blairstown, NJ, building three turbines which pumped water up a 200 ft tunnel to a mountain reservoir during the night and released the water in the morning to provide power. In all, he worked as a millwright for 25 years.

When Lottie suffered a paralyzing stroke in 1985, Dick dedicated his life 24/7 to her rehabilitation, which was agonizingly slow. After she gradually regained her ability to speak and walk, Dick bought a camper with which they travelled across the US in comfort. After twelve years of progressive improvements, Lottie relapsed, passing away in 1997. For Dick; however, life went on. He told me that since his grandmother died at age 93, his goal was to outlive her which, then at age 95, he had done with ease. In doing so, this quasi centenarian has become a treasure trove of memories of the good old days on Montana Mountain, when whiskey flowed like water and legendary figures lived out their colorful, eventful lives. After making my acquaintance and learning of my interest in this subject he told me to open the cabinet door under his kitchen sink, which to my surprise, I found was filled, not with cleaning liquids, but with whiskey bottles! He asked me to bring out a bottle of Laird's Applejack which I had already heard was made using the Smith family recipe. Then, telling me he would teach me how to drink whiskey, he filled two shot glasses ¾ full of whiskey and capped it with a bit of ginger ale. Ginger ale, he told me, killed the burn. The sharp bite of straight whisky, he said, could cause throat cancer; adding a bit of ginger ale prevented that.

Soon, words were flowing like spring water. At age 94, Dick said he had to make periodic doctor's visits. On one of them, the doctor asked him, "Do you smoke or drink?" Dick told him "I've never smoked, but I drink some." The doctor then routinely asked him, "how much?" Dick replied honestly, "well I usually have two shots of whiskey a day, but if I feel like more.... I'll cheat and have a helluva lot more"! The doctor smiled at his response and said, "Well, keep doing what you're doing... that's what's keeping you going!"

In response to my first query about who were the bootleggers on the mountain, Dick quickly responded saying, "First of all let me tell you, in the old days of Prohibition on this mountain everyone was a bootlegger. Everyone was involved in making moonshine." There were stills everywhere. Old man (Doyle) Styres (Dick's brother-in-law) who lived across from Pleasant Hollow Road had one hidden within a casement of cement blocks behind his house in the woods. Another one was down next to the saw mill below Dick's house and yet another was in a home once owned by Amzi Smith, built into an embankment behind the Pleasant Hollow School. Les Steele (Walt Steele's father), once a committeeman for Harmony, who lived down the road also made applejack. Those who were bootleggers did well financially and often became rich; those who weren't lost their farms. It was as simple as that. Times were tough back then, especially after the stock market crash of 1929.

Everyone had a gallon of whiskey in the trunk of their car. Apart from apples, corn and rye were also used. Dick's father used to get his whiskey from Tony Zielinski who lived with his wife Polly near Ingersoll Dam where the Merrill Creek Reservoir Visitor's Center is now located. Once when Rufus sent his sons to the Zielinski farm for a few bottles, Tony was out of stock, so he took Dick and his brother Henry in his touring car to Ralph Duckworth's farm where a supply was available. Dick said the Duckworths and Schanzlins were also bootleggers, but they were more discreet and less known than the Smiths. In those days, a quart bottle of applejack sold for $1 to $2. By the end of

Prohibition, he remembers the last bootleg whiskey he bought going for $12 a gallon. At this point, Dick paused to refill our shot-glasses and with a smile said, "You know, the drunker I stay, the longer I get" a phrase he told me he often used at Dornich's tavern in Brainards. After we had another few sips he continued conjuring up the past.

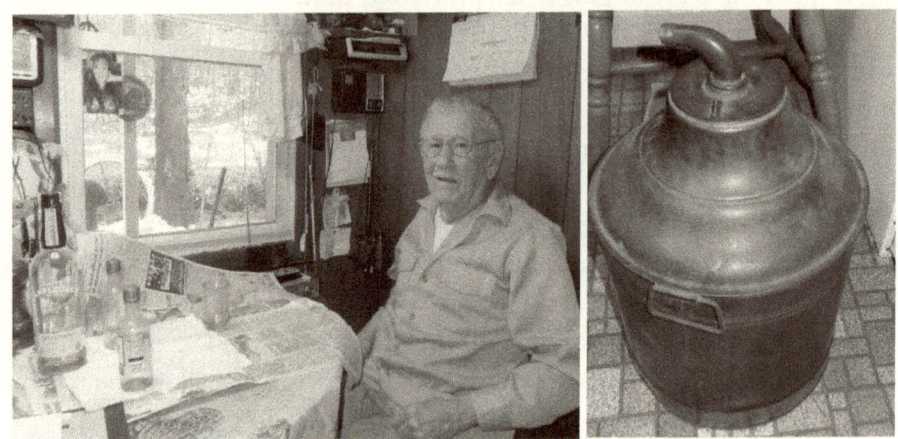

Left: Dick in his kitchen with a bottle of Lairds watched over by his lady friend.
Right: Dick's 5-gallon still.

Chapter Two
BOB CLOWER

According to Dick, Bob Clower, who came to Harmony from Easton around 1922, was "the King of the Bootleggers of Montana Mountain." He was a familiar sight at the nearby Warren County court in Belvidere where he would tell the judge "You know where I am and you know what I'm doing. When I get out, I'll go back doing just what I was doing before!" A former neighbor, Les Kober, remembers Bob being well educated. That isn't surprising considering at one point in October 1926 he announced to a judge that he would be his own defense lawyer![3] Bob's famed applejack was in high demand. Dick remembers that in the early 1920s, there was a signboard arrow nailed to a tree on every bend in the road on the mountain, which read "TO BOB'S." Anyone in search of hooch knew what the signs meant and followed them like a devout pilgrim to a shrine, which in this case was a house Bob rented from Steve Horvath in the wooded triangle junction of the Harmony Brass Castle Road and Fiddler's Elbow Road. The site, at the source of the Lopatcong Creek, was almost precisely where "D. Beer" had his apple distillery in the 1850s.[4] Bob lived there with his girlfriend, known as "Leaping Lena." Customers would enter Bob's place from a lane off Harmony Brass Castle Road and exit from the back of Bob's house onto Fiddler's Elbow Road. Bob was known to walk around carrying a 45 caliber pistol and thus was not a man to be trifled with. Dick remembered that the Stewartsville police once went up to raid him, but he chased them off. Parties at his house were

---

3 *Easton Express* article "Clower Would Be Lawyer" of 6 October 1926 p8 (see Annex 1); Judge Runyon; however, instead appointed a defense lawyer to represent him.
4 Ref: D.M. McCarty "Map of Warren County New Jersey", 1852.

common and were never dull. Men back then worked hard and partied hard. Women were plentiful and moonshine flowed liberally. Bob himself had been married twice. Dick remembered one occasion when a reveler got so drunk he was carried upstairs and laid across a feather mattress bed while Bob and his friends continued "raising hell" downstairs. At one point, Bob, in a celebratory mood, pulled out his pistol and started firing some rounds through the ceiling. Suddenly remembering the guy up on the bed, the revelers ran upstairs. Fortunately, the bullets missed him, but it was close: some of the mattress stuffing had been blown out leaving him covered with feathers! Apart from that, he was fine… sound asleep.

Bob's place was frequently raided by Fred Kroesen, a zealous, ubiquitous Prohibition Enforcement Officer. During a surprise raid on December 1st, 1923, Kroesen arrested Bob after finding and destroying two stills of 30 and 60-gallon capacity along with four barrels of what was described as "good stuff." In this instance, however, Bob got off the hook as the raid was launched without a search warrant.[5] On the 7th of the same month, Bob was fined $150 as a 1st offender after pleading guilty of illegal possession and sale of liquor and "three bottles of perfectly good red likor" were destroyed in court by pouring their contents into a washbasin.[6] Kroesen was relentless. In January 1924, he again raided Bob's place when Bob was absent and confiscated a 100 gallon still, two more of 50 gallons each, and destroyed 16 barrels of mash by mixing it with oil.[7]

Bob's son John was a bootlegger too. He lived just below the Smith's Sheeprock farm that Rufus had bought from Charlie Stukey in 1918. When Rufus found his cellar filled with empty bottles after moving to the area, he took the empty bottles to John who made good use of them and they soon became good friends. John lived with three women, one of whom was known as "Towpath Kitty" due to her familiarity with the bargemen on the Morris canal towpath at the foot of the mountain. Dick Smith remembers as a young boy one of these women, a heavyset gal, holding him on her lap and, in his words, "teasing the hell out of me." Eventually John married Towpath Kitty and they left

---

[5] *Easton Express*; "Still Raided at Montana"& "Federal Agent Acted First" December 3rd & 4th 1923 p8 (see annex 1).

[6] Ibid. "Clower Pays Fine for Violating Prohibition Law" December 7th 1923 p8 (see annex 1).

[7] Ibid. "Clower Place Raided Again" January 26th 1924 p8 (see annex 1).

for California never to return. Prior to John's move though, Bob would often set off walking over the mountain past Kober's junk yard with a gallon jug of whisky to his son's house and in passing would invite Rufus Smith to share a drink from his jug. Bob liked to compare the quality of his son's whiskey to his own.

By March 1924, Steve Horvath wanted his house back and Bob thus had to move. He soon found just what he wanted: a secluded house located on the other side of the mountain between Kober's junk yard and the Sheep-rock farm off Montana road opposite the home of Liege (Elijah) Woolf. It was here, where Bob made his last stills; some in his house, others hidden in the thickets by a swamp, which had the advantage of cold, clean spring water. It was also here that he was dubbed the "Lows Hollow Desperado," after another clash with his nemesis Kroesen who he shot through the sleeve during a tussle before Bob made a speedy exit dodging five bullets on the way out. The local press article commented: "that Clower is not charged with murder is due to his poor marksmanship"![8] Despite losing another 50 gallon still, Bob remained undeterred and soon built another one. Luck was again on his side when, in January 1925, the case against him for manufacture of intoxicating liquors and assault on Kroesen was dismissed since the raid was again undertaken without a search warrant.[9] Kroesen hadn't learned his lesson...

Bob then enjoyed almost two years of operational tranquility after his acquittal, in part, to his relief, due to Kroesen's resignation by July of that year. Always the womanizer, Bob struck up a relationship with a neighbor woman, known as "Felt Boot Mary" because of her footwear. Mary was often lonely when her husband went off for extended periods to work on other farms. With Bob nearby, she easily overcame her loneliness.[10] Bob's wild parties also continued at his secluded new place, which was not really a hideaway to those in the know. Eventually though, Bob's luck ran out, not from making liquor, but rather from drinking it. On August 22nd, 1926, he was arrested after crashing his car into a vehicle parked along the Belvidere Road in front of the home of George Clymer. Clymer and a visitor later testified that Bob seemed intoxicated and that after the accident he was attempting to

---

8 Ibid. "Bob Clower, Low's Hollow Desperado, Dodges Five Shots Fired at Him As He Ran From His Still" Mar 10th 1924 p8 (see annex 1).
9 Ibid. "Clower Case Dismissed" p8. January 30th 1925 (see annex 1).
10 Source: Dick Smith.

remove a jug of whiskey from his trunk, which Clymer took from him. After the Deputy Sheriff arrived on the scene, Bob denied that he had been drinking and swore he had no liquor in his trunk and that if any were found, someone must have planted it there! Charged with unlawful possession and transport of liquor Bob wanted to be his own lawyer at court, but the judge denied his request and appointed one to defend him. At the trial in October, the unlawful transportation charge was dropped but the charge of unlawful possession of liquor stuck and he was remanded to jail for sentencing. One of the arresting officers was asked at the trial if he had tasted the liquor and he replied that he had, and that "it was bum stuff." [11]

In May 1930 Bob was again pleading not guilty to an indictment charging him with unlawful manufacture and possession of intoxicating liquor, this time as a third offender. Again, he announced that he would defend himself, and although this time his wish was granted, Bob did not excel in his debut as a lawyer... The jury found him guilty and on June 6th he was sentenced, at age 55, to nine months in jail and ordered to pay a $500 fine. Released in March 1931, he did exactly as he always told the judge he would do: he went back to doing what he was doing before he went in! There was never a dull day with Bob.

Dick recounted to me that at one party at Bob's house a big fight erupted between Bill Lambert of New Village and another man and that one of them was stabbed during the fight. He remembered Bill as a strapping young man who worked in the nearby woods with his parents cutting trees and hewing them into railroad ties. Bill, Dick said, never wore shoes...only overhauls. He would drive the horses carrying the ties off the mountain and was considered lazy and worthless. In New Village, he was, in fact, known as the town drunk. Dick vividly remembered the fight as big news in the local press with headlines, which he thought read something like "Bad Man From Montana Stabbed Someone." He also remembered that despite the notoriety of Bob's place, a number of prominent and "respectable" personalities were present, enjoying Bob's hospitality when the embarrassing incident occurred.

As Dick could not remember the exact year it happened, I assured him that I would review every issue of the local Easton Express newspaper during the thirteen year Prohibition period until I found the

---

11 Ref *Easton Express* article "Clower Convicted" of 14 October 1926 p8.

article. After going through twelve years of newspapers, finally, there it was on the screen in front of me! Dated July 12th, 1932, the headline read "Giant Held for Stabbing Oxford Youth at Clower Mountain Home." The article described how William Lambert, 41 years old, of New Village, "tipping the scales at not less than 230 pounds," was charged with assault in the stabbing Clarence Miller, 21 years old, of Oxford. Lambert later claimed there was a free-for-all and that he was merely defending himself. Nevertheless, one from the group, a Lawrence Kappler, drove Miller to Warren hospital where a broken knife blade was removed from his body. In route to the hospital, Kappler ran into a bank, partially wrecking his car resulting later in a drunken driving charge. A Mr. and Mrs. Edwin Brown of Oxford were enjoying Bob's hospitality when the melee took place.[12] Two weeks later, on August 4th, it was reported that State Police "visited" the Clower place and upon crawling through his bedroom window, found "Big Bob" asleep with his pistol nearby. Waking up, Bob said he was expecting their visit and soon, after a big still along with a stash of wine and whiskey was discovered, he was taken to the jail in Washington.[13] On August 17th the curtain came down again on Bob when Judge Runyon sentenced him to another nine months in jail along with another $500 fine.[14]

By mid-May 1933, Bob was again a free man. Once again, he built a still which he carefully concealed in the brush of the swamp near his home. Then, on one unfortunate day the bush near the swamp caught fire and his new still blew up. It was to be his last, as Bob soon thereafter relocated off the mountain down to New Village, never to return.[15]

---

[12] See *Easton Express* Jul 12th 1932 p 8 (see excerpt in annex 4). Both Lambert and Kappler received served prison time.
See also: *The Phillipsburger* article "New Village Man Held Following Stabbing Affray" of 14 July 1932 in which the driver's name is indicated as "Keppler" instead of "Kappler".
[13] Ibid. August 4th 1932 p.8 NJ News (see annex 1).
[14] Ibid. August 18th 1932 p.8 NJ News (see annex 1).
[15] Source regarding the still blow-up and Bob's move to New Village: Dick Smith.

Chapter Three

THE KOBERS, MAGNANTES, GHETTIS, & WESTERS

The Kobers were among the biggest bootleggers on the mountain. Gabriel "Gabe" Kobor, born in 1881, and his wife Susan (née Fazekas) Kobor, who immigrated to the US from Hungary, bought their Montana Road farm in the early 1920s from Charlie Magnante, a Sicilian, who lived there with his wife and four sons. Les Kober remembered that Charlie made a lot of wine.[16] After selling the farm, Charlie moved to New York City where, as an accomplished accordion player, he became wealthy, in part, by playing in live performances at weddings, other dance venues and on radio and television. Back on the farm, Gabe who Anglicized his Hungarian name Kobor meaning "wanderer" to "Kober" soon followed his neighbors' example by supplementing his farm income by distilling bootleg whiskey. This decision was made easy and most likely encouraged by Magnante after Gabe found his basement full of not only old wine bottles, but also whiskey bottles, "oodles of them" according to Les, along with crock jugs and considering the large apple orchard on the property was already producing between 30 to 40 barrels of cider a year. The Kobers, like Rufus Smith, did not own a cider press and thus transported their apples by wagon to one nearby, in this case, in New Village. Gabe's son, Les, commented to me that hard drink was available at the mill and if one

---

16 As did many Italian families who were not about to change their cultural culinary habits because of Prohibition. Giacomo "Jack" Zocchi who lived off the mountain in Harmony Station would go to Modesto Calif. every year and ship a freight car load of grapes back to Phillipsburg, where he would take home what he needed for his own domestic use and sell the rest. In February 1929, three barrels of his wine made for domestic use were confiscated by local authorities and a fine was imposed.

over indulged, no worries.. The horses knew the way home.

Despite moving to New York City, Charlie Magnante maintained close ties with his beloved mountain, regularly making return visits to his former farm and homestead in his fancy Lincoln limousine which young Les remembers having wooden wheels and looking to him "like an undertaker's car." Ostensibly, Charlie came to visit his son, Charlie Jr., who still rented a cabin to the rear of the property.[17] On his departure; however, his limo was always filled to capacity with old Gabe Kober's white lightning.[18] Music was therefore not the only source of Magnante's wealth. It did however become that of Charles Jr. who, at age seven, secretly taught himself to play accordion using his father's instrument in his father's absence. Charles Jr. eventually rose to perform on the radio, television and reputably, before President Roosevelt at the White House. Amazingly, this Charles is now considered by many to be the most finished accordion player of all time. Apart from his performances broadcast over the air, he once performed before an audience of forty-thousand.[19]

Les Kober remembers that his father also made shipments of his own. Responding to orders from New York, he would stack up 25 to 30 square metal cans in the truck and deliver them to the insatiable city market, most likely under the wing of Magnante Sr.. Les remembered that during the early period of Prohibition his father's operation went smoothly and unmolested. In fact, he told me that Levi Mackey, who served as Sheriff from 1926-29, would occasionally drop in for a visit and leave with several gallons of whiskey. This cordial relationship was soon to change with Mackey's successor, Mansfield Bowers.

Les described his family's house to me as having three chimneys that merged to one outlet on the roof. The mash was stored in large wooden vats in the basement and these vats had to be occasionally cleaned. During the cleaning, the waste liquid was poured out on the grass and would flow into the pasture and down the hill. Their cows

---

[17] Charles Magnante Jr. amazingly became one of the most accomplished accordion players in music history. His performances with the *Charles Magnante Trio* can still be seen today on YouTube! Les also vividly remembers Charlie's older brother Angelo giving him a nickel every time he would say the word "shit"!
[18] During at least one of these extended return visits the Magnantes organized an instrumental/vocal concert at the Montana schoolhouse. Ref: *The Washington Star* article "Montana" of 14 Aug 1924 p8.
[19] see: http://www.accordions.com/memorials/mem/magnante_charles/index.shtml regarding the fame of Charles Magnante Jr. Source regarding his performance at the White House: Les Kober, who remembers reading about it in a newspaper at the time.

would then get drunk from drinking the mash waste as would those of their neighbor, Dewitt Wolverton, who apparently complained to the authorities.

Then came the day that Les vividly remembers, when Prosecutor Sylvester Smith suddenly showed up at their house with Sheriff Bowers and discovered the mash. "Got you now!" the Sheriff said to Gabe, "You're good for a couple years!" Things looked bad… that is, until the Sheriff and Prosecutor walked up to the back of the barn to inspect further. When they got there, their eyes popped! There, sprawled out on the hay in the barn, were three State Troopers, stone drunk!!! It was an all too embarrassing a situation to be in, and so the authorities appropriately decided that the best option was to give Gabe a stern warning this time and to tactfully retreat till another day. After that incident; however, the police kept the Kober farm under their constant radar.

Dick Smith remembers old Gabe Kober always having a Mason jar sitting on the floor next to his chair filled with a clear liquid,.. like water. Gabe's whiskey was never colored like that of his neighbors, thus meriting the name white lightening... Gabe would also regularly smoke cigarettes and throw the butts on the floor for his devoted wife Susan to later clean up. As a young boy Dick would spend a lot of time at the barbershop in New Village which was a local hangout (haircuts cost 50 cents back then …). As it got dark and he began the walk back up the steep hill to his home on Montana road he remembers the straining engines of trucks regularly passing him loaded with sugar for the local distillery operations either at the Kobers, Duckworths or multiple other destinations.

Dick also remembers as a child going for parties at the Kobers' house with his parents when old Ms. Kober would take him upstairs and put him in a warm feather tick bed and would later come to wake him up when the party was over. Gabe Kober, like Bob Clower, was well known for the quality of his product. This reputation eventually led him, like Bob Clower, to the courthouse. The day his luck inevitably ran out was reported by the local press on July 19th 1930 when during a raid, in which two men were found operating a still (of 1,000 gallon capacity!) on Gabe's farm. The still, unusually large for its type (for making rye whiskey) was equipped with all modern appliances for efficient operation including a steam boiler and large vats. The three were then arrested and held for trial with bail fixed at $1,000 bail each.

Unable to furnish bail, they awaited trial in jail. At the subsequent trial of January 18th 1931 the still operator, a man named Rude Madrigal, was fined $150 while Gabe and the helper, Daniel Devick, were fined $100 each.[20] After this unpleasant experience, there were no further public reports of bootlegging on the Kober farm..

Another Hungarian family on Montana Mountain was active during Prohibition besides the Kobers, and Wester Road in Harmony carries its name. The Westers seem, in fact, to have performed a feat of one-upmanship on the Kobers in the moonshining business! During a spectacular raid on February 22nd 1930 Emerick Wester, his three sons Andrew, Victor, John and another man were arrested when a huge 1,500 gallon still was discovered on their Harmony property in a barn about 30 feet from Emerick's house. A local press article[21] stated that "the still was modern and complete in every detail... operated with a steam boiler", the setup being "scientifically arranged". Apart from the still and boiler, "the raiders found two huge cooling vats on the top floor and on the second floor were six huge wooden vats eight feet deep and 12 feet wide. Three more similar wooden vats were found on the first floor." Also found were "26 five gallon cans of alcohol, 10 bags of corn sugar, 15 boxes of yeast containing 50 pounds each and a lot of alcohol in various containers not yet placed in cans for shipment". When the officers arrived, they also found "liquor running in a stream as thick as a man's finger." The same article reported a raid at the Bianco farm at the nearby Ingersoll dam where a non-operational still was found and confiscated. Emerick and Victor Wester later pleaded not guilty to three counts of illegal possession of liquor, illegal possession of a still and illegal manufacture of liquor while bail was set at $1,000 each. Ironically enough, at the same time this arrest was reported, a gentleman by the name of George Washington also pleaded not guilty in a case of illegal possession of alcohol.[22]

Then there were the Kinnemans, or rather the Italian Ghettis. Rita (Ghetti) Kinneman and her husband moved to Harmony from Washington, NJ where her husband worked with Kinneman Storage

---

20 *Easton Express/Easton Argus* articles "Big Stills Raided by Police In Warren County; Four Men Arrested" of July 19th 1930 p8, and "Fines of $850 paid in Court" of January 17th 1931. p8.
21 Ibid. article "Seize Huge Still In Montana Above Harmony; Arrest 5 Persons" of February 24th 1930 p8.
22 Ibid. article "Clower to Fight Case/ Pleads Not Guilty and is held for Trial" of May 8th 1930 p8.

and during the 1920s lived next to Rufus Smith's farm on Montana road in the home of Rita's parents Benelda and Cleto Ghetti. The Ghetti couple had nine other children besides Rita. Rita was one of six daughters. Dick remembers their mother walking up the road to visit them trailing her daughters like a mother goose followed by her line of goslings… Cleto he said had a brother Chero who once ran a bar called "Toots Tavern" on Sitgreaves Street in Phillipsburg, near where Warren Pipe and Foundry is now. This tavern provided a ready outlet for Cleto's homemade applejack production. One day however, while walking down the road to New Village, Dick saw a number of police cars in front of the Kinneman/Ghetti house. This event marked the end of this family's moonshine operation. Rita Kinneman had two sons who later moved to Florida and two daughters. Her husband had a problem with alcoholism. Her brother Dalio eventually sold the family home. Benelda Ghetti passed away much before her husband Cleto who Dick remembers as being "too mean to die". After the home was sold, he moved to Washington where he ended up passing away in a room in the St. Cloud Hotel. Rita became very close to Dick Smith after the passing of Dick's wife Lottie. Her husband had left her by then and she had a very difficult time raising their four children alone. The two remained very close until Rita herself passed away in July 2006 at the age of 82.[23]

---

23 Source of information on the Kinneman and Ghetti families: Dick Smith.

Chapter Four

THE BLOWUP, THE FOHRS, OLD MAN WILLIAMSON, & THE RICHLINES

Charlie and Charlotte Richline's house at the intersection of Richline Road and Allen's Mill Road was torn down in 2012. All that is left to mark the spot today is a heavily rusted wrought iron fence. Their old homestead dated from the Revolution, being built back in 1785. Its cellar was once a cooper shop and later a bakery with a brick oven where bread was sold.[24] Charlie, born in 1901, lived in the house for many years with his family having obtained it on the death of his father-in-law, old man John Williamson. Williamson obtained the property from Ingersoll Rand which procured extensive property there around 1903 on which it built a dam. He had earlier lived in a house lower down Harker's Hollow off Ragged Ridge but after losing it due to his inability to pay the $200 he owed on his mortgage, Ingersoll came to his rescue, deeding him the house and property free-of-charge in compensation for his services to the company in planting pine trees and as watchman for the dam. Old man Williamson was an active bootlegger having been raided by Sheriff Bowers on April 10th 1930 and he spent some time in jail in default of $800 bail after his 22 gallon still was found along with two 50-gallon barrels of mash and 10 gallons of liquor was found by the sheriff and confiscated. The still was in a tent in a hollow in the woods about a quarter mile from his

---

[24] Along with the house, a small stone arch bridge about 100 yards down the road from it which predated the revolution was also demolished to facilitate access for the heavy construction equipment needed to build the reservoir and with its destruction a piece of history was lost forever. Source: Carl "Corky" Richline.

house.[25] His son-in-law Charlie, who he didn't get along with, may have facilitated this arrest. When Charlie and Charlotte passed away, their property was purchased by the Merrill Creek Reservoir Owners Group.

Left: Charlie Richline. Right: The old Revolutionary era Richline homestead before its demolition (photos courtesy of Carl "Corky" Richline).

Before the Richlines and old man Williamson, however, in the early days of Prohibition, Dick remembers that a man, whose name he's now forgotten, lived there.[26] This earlier bootlegger kept his still in his house. One day while tending it, it blew up, scalding him badly. The man then ran down the road to his neighbors John and Amelia Fohr's house, about an eighth of a mile away (holler distance) for help. After telling his story the man pleaded to not be taken to the hospital because he would be arrested and jailed for his illegal activity. The Fohr's therefore kindly took him in, tended to his wounds and nursed him back to health. His stay was extended and extended to the point where he made their house his home having been taken on as a hired hand to further assist him. Eventually however he wore out his welcome and abruptly left his benefactors saying as he went out the door, "I'm going, there ain't no sense in me staying here no more" and away he

---

25 *Easton Express/Easton Argus* article "Raid Mountain Still; Arrested Man Jailed" of April 11th 1930 p8 and *The Washington Star* article "Still Near Harmony Visited by Officers" of 17 April 1930 p1.
26 Carl "Corky" Richline, John Stasyshun, and Bill Shepherd also remember him and believe his family name was Rush.

went never to return. By another account he was actually thrown out.[27] Dick remembers this man to be ornery and unpleasant; he met him once while walking through the woods and, when he went up to him, the man became irate with him because Dick had interrupted his aim at a groundhog. After the house passed through Williamson to the Richlines, Charlie began accumulating land for woodlots. All wood had a ready market, but Charlie sought out one species in particular which was more valuable: Chestnut wood. Despite the blight twenty years earlier, Chestnut trees still stood. Their wood didn't rot and, when burned, it didn't smoke, making it perfect for illicit bootlegger operations. Charlie thus supplemented his living as a steam shovel operator at the Edison Cement Plant by hauling it in his 1928 one-ton stake bed truck to a ready market. He never kept the deeds for his land purchases and in this profitable business made good friends, one of which was Walt Smith to whom he sold a wood lot. It was a lasting friendship.[28] Amazingly, like his friends Walt, Harry, and Dick Smith, Charlie Richline was also a mountain marksman. His family still remembers him standing long ago at the riverside shooting gallery in the now defunct Bushkill Park in nearby Easton where shooters paid 25 cents for 7 shots at tin cans hanging from strings a significant distance away. Charlie took a Winchester 22cal pump gun and one by one all seven cans fell to the ground, not by hitting the can, but by hitting the string each hung from! [29] As a close friend of the Smith brothers, he was also most certainly involved in the bootlegging business too. As late as the 1960s his grandsons remember him having six wooden kegs in the barn and as kids making money by buying cider from their granddad and then reselling it door to door at a significant profit.

The Richline's neighbor, John J. Fohr (whose parents came to the rescue of the earlier occupant of their house) also became a notable bootlegger. John's parents immigrated to the US from Hungary in 1905 and he was born on the mountain the following year. He later attended the one-room Montana schoolhouse where he was charged with starting the school's pot belly stove in the winter. He loved to tell the story of the day when one of the stove's legs broke and the students had to quickly run outside to gather snow to put out the fire. John

---

[27] Story as told by Dick Smith and also recalled by Bill Shepherd.
[28] Source: John Stasyshyn. The use of Chestnut wood as fuel for stills was also recounted to me by Dick Smith and was confirmed to me by others including Terry Lee.
[29] Source: John Stasyshyn.

later had the distinction of being the first person on the mountain to own a Model A Ford. As a pickup, it was of great use to him in transporting his bootleg off the mountain to New Village, a transit point, where it had a ready market. [30] He later recounted that on one such run his Ford, fully loaded with quart jars of moonshine, ran off Montana Road into the woods next to a stream. He fortunately found help to get the vehicle out of the woods and miraculously not one of the quart jars broke! The load was thus delivered to the scheduled drop off point where a middleman waited to transfer it to another conveyance off to Newark and New York City. John later recalled that he was a nervous wreck that day.[31] In another incident illustrating the hazards of such work, when cranking his Model T Ford to take another load of liquor off the mountain, the crank bar hit John in the jaw which left him with a permanent scar.[32]

---

30 Dick once told me that a Warren County Sheriff named Eckert lived in New Village. He had a Model T. coupe. His brother Jack (John) had a hotel there and lived with an older brother Steve. Across from the hotel was a General Store owned by Conrad Gruver. Dick told me the milk (and whatever else accompanied it) was unloaded at the store for transfer to its final destination. Later I learned that there was indeed an Eckert who was Sheriff of Warren County from New Village. His name was George Eckert who served from 1917 to 1920. Having a Sheriff as a brother might certainly carry with it certain advantages... After finishing his term I learned that George Eckert returned home to New Village to help his brother run his hotel which he took over on his brother's death.(ref *Easton Express article* of 4 January 1935 "Nine Former Sheriffs of Warren County Still Living"p8. The hotel and store were never raided during Prohibition despite the raids on the many families around them.
31 As told by John Fohr to his son-in-law Bill Shepherd.
32 As told by John Fohr to Steve Ignatz III and remembered by Steve's daughter, Mary Ann Ignatz.

Chapter Five

THE SMITH BROTHERS: WALT, HARRY, & CLARENCE

On another day of reminiscing, Dick told me about his Smith neighbors. Walter "Walt" Smith had charisma and was a character fondly remembered by those who knew him. He and his brother Harry were, in fact, Dick's best friends. Born on New Year's Eve 1896 Walt was the eldest of seven sons (there were also six daughters) of Adam S. Smith. Since Adam's wife Edith (Crane) was known as "Eve" it is often said among the family today that Adam and Eve were Smiths! Walt was perhaps the most colorful of the sons and was always a welcome patron at the local bars, as he loved to drink and have a good time. He became famous not just for his applejack but for his marksmanship. On Sundays as a young man, Walt would lay on his back in the middle of the then dirt road in front of Ropie's "Brainards Café" with his .22 caliber rifle in hand and, for a drink, betting anyone that he could hit any penny they threw high in the air. There were many takers. Onlookers inevitably gathered and inevitably jaws would drop amidst gasps as Walt shot penny after penny out of the sky without seeming to take aim...! He called it instinct. He and his brother Harry both had it just as Dick had told me he had it. Walt also loved to yodel and after a day of fishing his musical voice was often heard echoing up and down the Delaware River outside Joe McDermott's Oakhurst Café in Hutchison, his favorite hangout. Joe had earlier owned a bar at the corner of North Broad and 3rd streets in the Phillipsburg Flats near where, in January 1938, the New (Toll) Bridge was built. It was called "The Club House Café" and apart from booze, it featured activities such as boxing matches in the basement.[33] Joe's girlfriend was initially sent to run the Oakhurst until he moved there

---
33 Source regarding boxing in the basement of the Clubhouse Café: Wayne Deremer.

himself after selling the Club House Café in the late 1930s. Dick told me one day that during Prohibition Joe had also operated a pipeline that carried high powered beer from Easton, under the Delaware River into New Jersey where it was put in kegs and bottled. As this seemed a bit farfetched, I suggested to Dick that it was more likely that it was conveyed across by row-boat or over a ford in the river at night.[34] After all, I thought to myself, the mind can play tricks on a man in his mid '90s. Joe and Walt were however birds of a feather, and best of friends. At the Oakhurst, apart from his yodeling, Walt was also known to give stellar performances imitating Red Skelton which would bring laughs to any gathering.

Walt's first passion was however his bootleg whisky operation which he ran from his farm on Harmony's Ridge Road which had a large stream-fed pond in the front of the house and a large barn to the side. With one of his stills carefully hidden in his basement, Walt's barn was used to store his essential ingredients: sugar and cider, which were secretly kept behind a special partition. An underground pipe conveyed the cider to the basement of the house where it was distilled into the final product and stored in oak barrels. Walt always seemed to be praising his wife, the former Rosa Steele, who somehow tolerated him over the years. He was thus always saying to his friends "I married my Rosa and I love her still", a double entente which always generated chuckles since Rosa also spent time in the basement keeping an eye on business. One of Walt's cousins, Joe Smith of Hutchison, remembers as a boy going inside Walt's barn and seeing long lines of gallon whiskey bottles wrapped and arranged neatly in rows on the floor ready for a delivery. Others remembered seeing trucks loaded with sugar and cider drive up behind the barn during their visits and being asked to help unload them. The operation continued throughout Prohibition and was never uncovered.

When he wasn't spending his pastime livening up a bar, Walt might be either out hunting coons, foxes, or deer or otherwise be out fishing on the river. He knew every fishing hole on the Delaware and would dismiss complaints about poor fishing in the river by saying the fish were there, you just had to know where to look and how to catch them.

---

[34] I later found out that a ford across the Delaware River did in fact exist between Easton and Phillipsburg. Known as "The Cattle Crossing" it was situated just below the mouth of the Lehigh River near where the Kuebler Brewery was located and therefore may have been used to convey alcohol across the river during Prohibition (Source: Bruce Schofield).

Walt loved to hunt and Dick Smith would often accompany either Walt or his brother Harry or both. When they went hunting, Walt and Harry would always have to have some whiskey first. No formality, just pass the jug around from person to person and take a swig or two. As already said, the three of them were all sharpshooters. Dick said matter-of-factly that he would routinely put a Victrola record up against a distant tree and shoot a 22 bullet through the center hole. They loved to go after coons and foxes with their prized fox hounds.

Left: Walt Smith at the Delaware River near the Oakhurst Café Walt with a prize fish in Hutchison (private collection). Right: Easton Express photo provided by Bruce Unangst and with permission of the Express-Times

On one occasion after taking some draughts from Walt's gallon jug they released their hounds near the pipeline on Ragged Ridge. Walt went down one side while Dick was on the other when a fox ran down and Dick shot it, remembering it "screaming like a woman". Walt was also screaming, "You shot me!! You SOB, you shot me!! I had only one good eye before and now have none!!" (in jest of course) Meanwhile, another fox ran into a hole. Dick remembers that Walt then performed an incredible feat. He got a long flexible stick and pressed it far into the hole, then saying "I feel him, I feel him!" he slowly pulled the stick out of the hole and the fox came out after the stick, but bolted off after seeing them with the dog in hot pursuit. The dog then grabbed the fox and Walt grabbed the dog and the dog eventually killed the fox. The foxes were then skinned and the pelts sold.

Once Walt shot a doe on the mountain during Buck season and was carrying the carcass on his back over a ridge. Coming across some hunters he said "You damned hunters shoot these deer and us wardens have to carry em in". After putting the deer in his trunk Walt then came across a real warden who asked him "Have you seen any deer up here?" Walt's reply was quick, "there ain't no damned deer up here at all". [35]

Back in Brainards, this time at Dornichs' tavern run by John and Ethel Dornich next to the railroad tracks, Walt's drinking companions remember him staggering out of the bar one night, going over to the railroad tracks, and falling asleep in the middle of the tracks. He also had wild parties at his house on Ridge Road and would entertain his guests with his singing and yodeling. Walt had a few animals on his farm, mainly goats, along with a horse and a donkey. People would stop while driving by to see the animals and their kids would often ask him, "What's the donkey's name?" Walt's reply was always the same: "His name is Giddy up and Go!" Once Rosa hung her clothes neatly on the clothesline to dry and after going to the basement looked at the clothes line to find it empty: the goats had wreaked havoc in her absence dragging the clothes in all different directions in the pasture trying to make a meal of them. There was always something going on at Walt's house.[36]

Walt did a brisk business with his moonshine. Some of his production was sold direct from his farm to his friends on Sundays. One source estimates that it was nothing for Walt to make over $1,000 during one of these sales. Walt also made deliveries. The brother of Bill Nolan, the bartender at what was later known as George's Tavern on the Belvidere road used to drive Walt's shipments to the city in a car that had storage tanks under its frame. When he had earned enough money he bought himself a dark coupe similar to the type the Feds used which he proudly drove up to Walt's place to pick up a consignment. When he drove his new car up Walt's lane, Walt stood in the

---

35 Story as told by Dick Smith. As this incident may have occurred before Dick was drafted it is worth mentioning that Walt, his brother Harry and Claude Rudd were employees of the Lopatcong Water Company at that time and were appointed by the Harmony Township Committee as "Special Officers" of the Water Company where they worked as guards. Ref *Easton Express* article "Harmony Names Special Officers" of 17 April 1942 p8. Such official positions would likely have facilitated their hunting forays.
36 Source for this paragraph: conversation with Andy Thorpe 24 August 2013.

middle of it with a shotgun until he identified himself![37]

In August 1933, only four months before the repeal of Prohibition, Walt made the local news after being arrested and convicted on a drunken driving charge by Justice of the Peace Clark Willever of Washington. During the appeal at the county court, however, after it was determined that a physician did not examine him until four hours after his arrest, (these were pre-breathalyzer days) and moreover, since two witnesses denied he was intoxicated, the judge's decision was reversed.[38]

Walt's brother Harry born in April 1900 was four years his junior, but was just as renowned as his brother for his moonshine. Some in fact considered Harry's liquor better than Walt's. Harry moved to Harmony from Mt. Freedom in Morris County, NJ in 1925 at Walt's encouragement. By 1928 after living a few years next to his brother and mastering the art of distilling, he had bought a house of his own on the nearby Harmony Brass Castle Road and, like Walt, set up his own 75-gallon still in his basement. In those days the bootleggers would often carefully bury their production in barrels under the stones in stone rows. That was risky business however because if someone found such a cache (and many were out looking for them) they would steal it! Because apple cider was in plentiful supply, Harry, like most bootleggers, made mostly applejack although he would also make whiskey from wheat, barley and rye depending on what was available. The mash would often be placed next to his wood stove to ferment before distillation. Some moonshiners would take the easy route and make whiskey by simply setting cider out in the sun to ferment and become hard, after which the barrel was left out during the winter to freeze solid. A burning hot rod would then be tapped into the center of the barrel to extract the almost pure whiskey.

Harry had three boys. The eldest, Harry Lester, remembered rolling his father's whiskey barrels into storage. There was a constant flow of whiskey to Morristown near where the family had previously lived and people, including local State Troopers, were always knocking on the door for it at five dollars a gallon. Business remained brisk throughout Prohibition. Harry's eldest son told me that during this period he

---

[37] The source of this story wishes to remain anonymous. Although the make of this car is unknown, powerful six cylinder Packards and Hudsons known as "Whiskey Sixes" were the cars of choice of bootleggers. Hudson offered better suspension, steering gear and shock absorbers and later developed a "Super Six" which could easily outrun police vehicles.
[38] *Easton Express* article "Defendants Plead Guilty" of August 3rd 1933 p8.

remembered his father driving to Newark with a 60 gallon barrel in his car and getting $800 dollars for it! Surprised at the amount, I asked him who he sold it to, and he quickly replied, "the Chief of Police!" While that delivery went smoothly, but not all did. On another delivery run to Newark, Harry and a friend carried a truckload full of applejack cleverly covered with a thick layer of cinders to avoid detection. They were supposed to meet someone at a pre-agreed location who would tell them where to make the delivery. They never made it to their destination though. Soon after entering Newark a large fancy black limo forced them off the road onto the sidewalk. Some dangerous looking men then emerged from the car armed with guns and forced Harry and his helper out of the truck. The men then stole the truck and all its precious contents, leaving the two standing in the dust of their own cinders! The Mafia could have very well been involved and under the circumstances, considering the cargo, contacting the police would not have helped. The two thus simply had to find their way back home… empty handed.

Back at home, the local police, who would regularly come to Harry's house to buy their whiskey by the bottle, were certainly much less feared than the Feds or the mob. Nevertheless, as a young child during prohibition, Harry's daughter Arlene remembers often smelling burnt sugar in their house as a little girl and occasionally hearing her father shout out the strange words "Revenue Men!" after which he would quickly fly out the back door for the woods. It was only later that she learned what the words meant, about her father's still in the basement, and the 10 gallon barrels of whiskey stored under the floor of the old barn behind their house, which they called "the pig-pen".

Occasionally one of these pesky officials would fly over in a newfangled "autogiro", the precursor to aerial surveillance helicopter, but Harry's still was never found. The trick, as Harry learned from his brother Walt, was using Chestnut wood to fire the stills, since Chestnut wood doesn't smoke, and smoke would give away the still's location.

Harry's son Don remembers at age 26 going with his father to deliver a 10-gallon keg of applejack to a client in Belvidere. The customer would keep the keg in his car. There was always charcoal at the bottom of each keg. The whiskey from the bottom of the keg in direct contact with the charcoal, he said, was the best. Customers came from all social levels. Apart from the police, another important client who would occasionally drop in was a young lawyer named Bob Meyner of Phillipsburg, who later became the Governor of New Jersey. The big shots from Ingersoll Rand were also good customers. Prices ranged from $5/gallon during Prohibition to $12/gallon by the time it ended.

Autogiros of the type used to reconnoiter for illicit mountain stills during Prohibition (with permission of Donald A. Eckel).

Living just down the road, on the Pleasant Valley Road, Dick Smith knew Harry very well. In one conversation he told me that Harry didn't drink all the time, but once in a while he would decide "to go on a drunk". He would then fill up a jug and walk through the woods to Dick's house where he would knock on the door and stay until after midnight when Dick said he would have to politely throw him out. Once during the day he ran down through the woods to Dick saying "You have to help me hide my still, the revenuers are coming!" They then had to quickly hide it behind some rocks in the woods and any loose kegs and bottles were quickly stowed under the floor boards of his barn.

At this point, my conversation with Dick that day was interrupted by a phone call. I overheard the caller asking Dick "how ya doing?" his response was a quick: "Well, I'm still here!" The call was short and we were soon focusing again on the past.

Harry Smith (1900-1959) & his wife Dorothy (Huber) Smith (1900-1972) (Courtesy of the Smith family).

Chapter Six
THE SEARLES BROTHERS

Three of the Searles brothers: Beef, Witt, & Slim
(courtesy of Carl "Corky" Rich line).

Of the families who lived in and around Lows Hollow on Montana Mountain some are remembered not for their skills in producing prized whiskey but for their reputation for drinking it. They were colorful characters who gave flavor to the overall atmosphere and created folklore which lives on to this day. The Searles boys were such characters. There were four Searles brothers, known as "Beef", "Witt", "Slim", and "Brick". They were huge boys and all grew up in a log cabin shack on Low's Hollow Road with their mother. Some wondered how they could all fit in there together. Three of them (Beef, Brick, and Slim) had fought in the trenches during the First World War and one faced Mustard Gas.[39] The younger ones, according to Dick Smith were "the

---
39 Source: John Stasyshyn. The Searles brothers are fondly remembered by the older residents of Montana Mountain.

good ones" and soon married and left home to begin lives of their own. Before they left however, Slim was hit by a car one evening after leaving the Franklin House in New Village in route to Conrad Gruver's general store across the street. The driver stopped and the boy was put in the back seat to be delivered to Warren Hospital, which the driver grumbled about because he didn't want his seat to get blood stained.

Unlike their younger brothers, "Beef" and "Witt" never left home, never married and continued to live with their mother. According to one source, the two "drank like hell".[40] Dick remembers them working on the top of the mountain on Tony Zilinski's farm. Once they came to his father's farm on a motorcycle with a side car partially filled with hard cider. They then filled the rest of the side car with cabbage which Dick's parents sold at 5 cents/head and off they went with one boy riding the bike and the other perched on the top of the cabbage. John Stasyshyun remembers that the brothers had two Indian motorcycles, one an Indian Chief 74. Although they later worked at Shillinger's Mill near Stewartsville, the occupation the two were most known for in the 1930s and 40s was grave-digging. They took no cash for this work; instead, their fee for digging a grave at the Stewartsville Lutheran Cemetery was one bottle of good whiskey.[41]

The Searles brothers were extremely strong. Les Kober remembers seeing Beef over at Ellis Apgar's cider mill one day and when Beef saw a 50 gallon barrel of hard cider he asked if he could have a drink. Ellis said, "OK, if you can lift it". Beef then sat on a step and, getting down on his knees, lifted the barrel up on his knees and drank out of it. Jaws dropped. In another dare, two of the Searles brothers were bet that they couldn't lift the Phillipsburg-Washington trolley off its tracks and so they went over to it and did just that.[42] They were also fearless. Witt liked to tell the story about the day his brother Beef was walking along the Lehigh River with friends when they came across a water moccasin snake. After someone bet his brother that he couldn't take the snake's teeth out he did just that but in the process was bit. Seconds later the snake was dead, smashed against the rocks and the brother cut an X on the bite and sucked the venom out while dousing the wound with whiskey.

---

40 Source: Dale Hamlen in a conversation of 19 November 2013.
41 Ibid.
42 As told to me by Claude Rudd.

Chapter Seven

CLINT HARTUNG OF ROXBURG & HIS NEIGHBORS LEO LOMMASON & JOHN PAVONI

Clinton "Clint" Hartung (1880-1971) is most remembered as being a successful farmer in Roxburg. Although he was not a bootlegger, Prohibition was a time when money could be made by anyone willing to take risks. Clint made regular trips to Canada to bring back cattle, but likely there may have been more being carried back in his truck on the return trip besides cattle.[43] Dick remembered Clint well. In fact, he worked with him hauling rock and landfill, which was unloaded behind the Lower Harmony Church on which the homes of Wes Garrison and Bob Vannatta were later, built. He only knew Clint, however, as a farmer. He also remembers Clint's father George pulling out onto the Belvidere road in his shiny new Cadillac. Clint's brother Charles of nearby Delaware, NJ was however a notable moonshiner who seized the opportunity to supplement his farm income and he would occasionally bring Clint samples of his production. Once Charles dropped in for a visit with a large parcel and Clint's wife Blanche who met him at the door asked what it was. On hearing what contents were she was quiet thereafter.[44]

The Hartungs' neighbor in Roxburg was an enterprising young man named Leo Lommason whose Prohibition activities directly affected them. Across from the Hartung farm stands a very old grist mill built on the Ragged Ridge Creek. It was built prior to the American Revolution by Captain Joseph Mackey who, in 1777, was commissioned Captain in the 1st Regiment of Militia of Sussex County and died in 1798 a prosperous miller. When Leo Lommason purchased this mill

---
43 Source: a family member who wished to remain anonymous; 14 August 2013.
44 Source: Tim Rue who was told the story by Clint and Blanche's daughter Gertrude.

around 1919 as a 30 year old man he modernized the old dilapidated equipment but, with Prohibition, illegal whiskey production became a much more profitable business than milling and so he shifted the focus of his attention to white lightening. As his mill sat just off the main road, however, revenuers soon began watching the facility and since neighbors Clint and Blanche Hartung had the only phone in Roxburg at the time, they received a written order to give Federal agents access to their line to coordinate a raid about which they were sworn to secrecy. So it was that late one quiet afternoon on January 4th 1933 while Clint and Blanche were attending a meeting at the Roxburg Grange at the foot of the Roxburg Hill, an explosion ripped through the air! To the Hartungs, it must have come as no surprise that the blast came from the old grist mill across the street. Everyone went running outside to find the millhouse slightly damaged but a huge 3,000 gallon still in pieces. The still was reported by the Feds to have been producing about 500 gallons of 195 proof alcohol per night. Although it lay less than 300 feet off the main road, a waste pipe was cleverly run about 100 feet up the hill to disperse the fumes. The equipment seized was mostly brand new. Leo and four others were arrested with bail set at $500 each. Revenuers also confiscated the elaborate equipment and broke open all the whiskey barrels, releasing the precious liquid which, along with the mash, flowed down the Grist Mill Road, across the Belvidere Road into Clint's dairy cow pasture. The cows there were not at all displeased by this tasty ooze and soon became pleasantly drunk. One can image them dancing the night away… Leo Lommason's fun, however, was over and his profitable operation came to an abrupt end.[45] At the time of his arrest, Leo was a respected member of the Harmony Township Committee on which he served from 1925-38 and also served his community as a member of the local Board of Education. The event and the big splash it made in the local press thus caused him considerable embarrassment. Coincidentally, the same page in the local press also reported the death on January 5th 1933 of former President Calvin Coolidge, whose Presidency (1923-29) spanned most of Prohibition which he staunchly supported. Prior to his death, however,

---

[45] The background to this story was taken with permission from *Bloodroot: 101 Dalmatians* by Tim Lewis Rue; Authorhouse Press 2009 p164-168. The event was also reported in *The Phillipsburg Star* newspaper article of January 6th 1933 p1 "Federal Officers Raid Big Still Near Roxburg" and in an *Easton Express* article of January 5th 1933 p8 under the heading "Raid Still Near Roxburg". The details in these two articles differ somewhat.

he confided to a friend, "I feel I no longer fit in with these times". Yes, times were changing.

Another of Clint Hartung's neighbors was John Pavoni, the owner/operator of the Roxburg Hotel, a lively place where men also got pleasantly drunk and whose esteemed patrons included Walt Smith. On March 3rd 1930 it was particularly lively when a police raiding party showed up at the door and found it securely locked. It took a while for the officers to gain entry but when they did, they hit a jackpot finding 30 barrels of hard cider along with beer and a still in a nearby barn all of which were confiscated. Pavoni and two of his patrons, Harry Bowers of Bangor, and William Hawk of Brainards were arrested: Pavoni for unlawful possession of liquor with a bail of $1,000 and the others respectively for resisting arrest and disorderly conduct as well as driving without a license. The article stated that Pavoni had conducted the hotel for a long time and was previously arrested for unlawful possession of intoxicating liquor. [46]

---

46 *Easton Express* article "Raid Made at Roxburg" of Mar 4th 1930 p8. Earlier, on April 19th 1928 the *Easton Express*, in an article *Defendants Enter Pleas* reported on a man named "John Paini" of Roxburg who pleaded guilty of possession of intoxicating liquors and paid a fine of $100.

Chapter Eight
THE DENKERS, THE BIERGARTEN, & THORPE'S GROVE OF LOW'S HOLLOW

The only known image of Christel Denker's Biergarten-early 1930s (Courtesy of Caroline Denker).

Christel Denker, born in Germany in 1879, immigrated to the US in 1893 at 14 years of age on board the HH "Meier" from Bremen. Although he came from a large family, he travelled alone. The reason for this is unclear although he went straight to Jersey City which might infer that he had family there. His future wife, Johanna Amalie Oertel arrived in New York five years later in 1898 at age 12 with her mother and sister Lidia "Liddy" to join an older sister, Fanny, who had preceded them and had found work as a personal maid to the Ellises, a wealthy New York family, that divided its time between their home on Park Avenue and another in the suburbs. Eventually Christel

Denker met and married Johanna and the couple lived in Jersey City where their first three children were born: Dorothy in 1906, Walter in 1909, and Christ in 1910. The couple moved to Harmony in 1916 settling near the foot of Ingersoll Dam on Lowes Hollow Road near Stewartsville where six more children were born: Violet in 1916, Lydia in 1920, Harold in 1926, Norman in 1927, Roy in 1928, and Johanna in 1930. Johanna's mother, known as "Oma" to the kids also lived with them.

Although he worked the night shift at Ingersoll Rand to support his large family it was difficult making ends meet; thus, after Prohibition was enacted in 1919 Christel joined his neighbors on Montana Mountain in a lucrative pastime which greatly supplemented his family income: bootlegging. Behind their house Christel had a small barn where he often spent time. Johanna knew what was going on, but minded her own affairs. They would however make regular visits to New York in the 1930s ostensibly to visit "Tunda Fanny" but also carrying a load of his whiskey which had a ready market through Mrs. Ellis's chauffeur who acted as the go-between with insatiable buyers. On the ride back, daughter Beatrice would much later recall the family having to sit on bags of sugar, an essential ingredient for the next batch. Life was good and the Denker children thrived despite the hardships related to the Depression.

Christel became well known for the "Biergarten" he organized in 1933 in a makeshift annex to back entrance room to the kitchen of his house in Low's Hollow just below the Ingersoll Dam. Saturdays were special days and the kids and Oma went to bed early. Beer and whiskey were publicly available there on Saturdays after Prohibition ended and dances were regularly held. Christel's son Chris who was a Square Dance figure caller at the Harmony Inn was happy to tend bar. [47]

In Low's Hollow at that time there was also a dance hall called Thorpe's Grove owned by Roy Thorpe and his wife Elsie which made the Hollow a lively place to be. Many would bring their own bottle. Walt Smith was a regular visitor and especially loved the clambakes the Thorpe's held there. Roy's nephew Andy who grew up on nearby Marble Hill Road remembers seeing drunken men running through the fields saying "have you seen the Moon tonight?" while dropping their drawers to expose their gleaming bottoms to the ladies.[48] After dark,

---

47 Sources regarding Cristel Denker: Caroline, Dick Denker, and Dick Smith.
48 Source: Andrew "Andy" Thorpe aka "Thorpy" son of Buck and Edith Thorpe; 24 Aug. 2013.

the revelry continued illuminated by kerosene lanterns and indoor toilets had not yet replaced outhouses. Occasionally there was a brawl. Dick Smith remembers a night when the constables came looking for trouble to arrest someone when a fight started. A big Italian named Utz "Jumbo" Guida tackled the cops and using Dick's words, "beat the hell out of them". The next day Dick said the State Police returned with warrants issued in the name of "John Doe" which they used to arrest anyone who might have been involved. A lawyer in nearby Washington, N.J. who was the magistrate at the time, later set everyone free.

Dick Smith remembers another night going with his mother for dinner to the home of Jim Cathers who lived near the Denkers. A Victrola provided the music, kerosene the lighting and after the party they had to go out to the barn to find the horse and buggy in the dark.

Up at the nearby Ingersoll Dam, the dam custodian, Earl Rudd, was well known to the travelers on Low's Hollow Road. Police raids up the Hollow were frequent during Prohibition. Apart from Bob's Place, liquor caches were seized at the homes of Thomas Bianco and Joe Uberseder and a still was seized on the Bianco farm in 1930.[49] With the construction of the Merrill Creek reservoir in 1988 much has changed, buildings are gone. A ride through the area with Dick however revives the past. An abandoned lane to the right before the entrance to the Merrill Creek Visitors Center is pointed out as going to where Tony and Polly Zielinski once lived. Tony passed away back in 1940. After the Zielinski farm was the property of Jim Cathers and after that was the Harvey Beers farm and on down Low's Hollow, the Denker home. Chris Denker was an old friend of Dick Smith and one of his frequent companions on coon hunts. Harvey Beers eventually bought the Zielinski farm which passed to his son Roy who ran the two farms while working as a night cleaner at a bank where one night he was found dead on the floor. Roy was known for his wild applejack parties.

Although the homes of the Denkers', Cathers', Zielinskis' and Beers' are now gone they and the stories of the families who lived in them remained vivid in Dick's memory and live on in the minds of those who remember the halcyon days of yore before the scenic dam was replaced by an immense reservoir which left many mountain homes and farms under water.

---

49 See *Easton Express/Easton* Argus articles entitled "Two Alleged Moonshiners Taken by Federal Agent" of May 8th 1925; p8 & " Seize Huge Still in Mountains Above Harmony" of February 24th 1930.

Chapter Nine
THE STEELES, THE UNANGSTS, THE APGARS, & THE OTHER SMITHS

In the halcyon days before cars and internet, young country folk would most often marry neighbor kids or school classmates since most were burdened with farm work and, with transport being by horse or foot, the normal travel radius was limited. The rural folk of Harmony Township's Montana Mountain were no different. Clint Hartung, for example, who lived in the flatlands below Montana Mountain, met his young wife Blanche in 1897 at the annual Warren Country Farmer's Picnic and would court her at her home on the Belvidere Road during his weekly wagon trips to Easton, PA to sell hay. The Steele, Unangst, and Apgar families are thus presented here under the same heading since these Harmony families are essentially kinfolk through intermarriage. Also allied with these families is another Smith line, equally as old as the notorious Smith brothers' line, both reaching into the distant past before the American Revolution.

Wendel Steele, born in Germany in 1832, settled with his wife Parmelia on Montana Mountain in the mid 1870s. The couple had three children: Mary, Joseph, and Rose. It wasn't long before Wendel was "in like Flynn" with his neighbors and enjoying the good times with them. In fact in 1894 he was convicted and fined $400 for running "a disorderly place" where he sold "choice wines of all kinds for 20 cents a quart".[50] His daughter Rose Josephine (1874-1946) married Amzi Smith (1872-1963) one of the godfathers of the bootlegging Smiths. Wendel's son Joseph and his wife Sarah raised their three children Rose E. aka "Rosa", Leslie "Les", and Joseph in a farmhouse which stood on the left side of the dirt "Richline Road" which once cut to the

---
50 "Gay Nineties in Warren County Selected Bits, Serious and Amusing from Files of Old Newspapers 1894" by Frank G. Andrews. *Easton Express* 11 Mar 1938 p8.

right off Harmony Brass Castle Road at Allen's Mills and meandered up the mountainside to Ingersoll Dam. Rosa (1895-1996) married the renowned Walt Smith whose oft repeated double entente "I married my Rosa and I love her still" always made folks chuckle. Les Steele later owned and operated a farm on the Harmony Brass Castle road just below Swamp Road which was just up from his uncle Amzi's orchards. Dick Smith knew Les Steele was a bootlegger, once telling me, "How could he not be, with Walt Smith as his brother-in-law and Amzi Smith as his uncle!?" Les, however, was discreet; after all, he became a Township Committeeman and was mayor for a time. After his daughter Verna Mae married Jay Unangst, Les sold the couple a plot of land at the corner of Swamp Road on which they build their home in 1948. Their home is now owned by their son Bruce who was born in 1957.

Jay Unangst, born in 1922, was one of three boys born to Frederick and Elizabeth Unangst of Stewartsville. His parents ran a cider press next to the Franklin House in nearby New Village. Dick remembered Jay well along with his brothers Eugene and Clair, known as "Horsey" and "Barker". Barker worked with Dick in the forge at Ingersoll Rand in Phillipsburg. "In their young days" Dick said, "those Unangst boys loved to drink and get into an occasional fight". Jay was a huckster; he would travel around from house to house selling vegetables and would also peddle some whiskey along with it for his father-in-law, Les. Dick remembers once seeing some laborers working on the oil pipeline that went up Ragged Ridge and back down across Harmony Brass Castle Road. It must have been in the early '30s. According to Dick, the pipeline, which consisted of two pipes, was built in the 1890s and ran from the oil fields in Pennsylvania over Ragged Ridge, through Broadway to a refinery in Passaic. The workers were repairing some leaks when Jay happened to pass by and began talking with them. Jay then said, "You fellas need a drink. Let me go get you one" and with that he shot off down the road to Les Steele's house. It wasn't long before he was back with a gallon of whiskey swinging from his hand. The offering brought smiles all around and laborious task at hand suddenly became a lot easier... in fact enjoyable.

In more recent times, Jay's son Bruce remembers as a young man finding an old bottle of whiskey with a pinecone floating in it in his father's liquor cabinet. Turning to his father he asked, "Dad, what's this stuff?" When Jay replied "that's a bottle of your mom's Uncle Walt Smith's famous applejack", Bruce was excited and asked if he could try some. Jay said, "Sure". Getting a wax coated Dixie cup Bruce was about to pour some into the cup when his father said "stop !" warning him that Walt's applejack was so strong it would eat right through the wax! With a glass therefore he tasted what he recalls being the best whisky he ever had. The reason for the pinecone being in the bottle remains a mystery, although it may have added to the taste. Bruce also remembers that during an American Legion Convention in 1975 his father took with him a 60-year-old bottle of "Seagrams Benchmark", a pre-prohibition bottle of 1915! Whereas a whiskey bottle in the 1970s had a cork, this one was a sealed bottle. Bruce was lucky enough to get a taste of it and said it was very smooth with a hint of charcoal, which immediately brought to my mind what Harry Smith's son Don had told me: that the best whiskey was at the bottom of the keg where it was in contact with the charcoal.

Going back in time, after Wendel Steele's daughter Rose Josephine married Amzi Smith, she brought with her a child named Henry Steele, known as "Hank". Although Amzi could at times be testy with Hank, he accepted him as his own giving him a plot of land adjoining his up a private lane off Ridge Road near Wendel's farm on which Hank built a shack, where he lived. Behind the shack was a barn and behind the barn, at the crest of the mountain ridge, was an apple orchard. Amzi's son Elwood built a ranch home on Ridge Road at the entrance to this private lane, which put him somewhat in the position of a gatekeeper.

Hank quickly picked up the art of bootlegging from his stepfather. Dick Smith remembers his friend Harry Smith once telling him that he was once over at Hank Steele's shack making whiskey and they urgently needed a strainer to strain it but there was none ready at hand. Hank was an improviser; running quickly to the corner of his shack, he grabbed an old pair of his dirty work pants and tore out a pocket which served the purpose very well! This was a bit unorthodox for Harry who was meticulous in his distilling processes, but for Hank, what his clients didn't see wouldn't hurt them. Dick remembered another interesting story about Hank's unorthodox hooch handling techniques- one in which he was personally involved. Hank and Harry had sold a 10 gallon keg of whiskey to a fellow in Phillipsburg, but since he defaulted on payment, they went to him and took the keg back. On their way home they stopped at Dick's place and wanted to give him a gallon but they had nothing with which to siphon the whisky from the barrel into a jug. In the end, Dick's wife Lottie came to the rescue, providing them with one of her douche bags for the purpose. Dick says it was the best whiskey he ever had!

Despite occasional payment defaulters, Hank's moonshine business was nonetheless very profitable and by April 1920 he and his wife Hattie (Rasley) had built and moved into a bungalow across the street from Garrison's "Harmony Garage" where they also ran an attached convenience store.[51] This most likely would not have been possible with Hanks income from his job at Ingersoll Rand alone. Their home still stands to this day. Alas, liquor also proved to be Hank's downfall. At one point Hattie got so frustrated and angry that she threw Hank's mattress out of the upstairs window of their cottage onto the garage roof which sent Hank into seclusion in his shack. Hank later ran off with a young gal to Florida where he squandered whatever money he had. Eventually he returned home penniless spending the remainder of his days a broken man. When Hank passed away, his daughter Frances was embarrassed that there were no decent clothes in which to bury him. In the end, Viola (Simons) Cruts, a dear friend and neighbor, came to the rescue providing them with a suit which had once belonged to her father Arthur so that Hank would look presentable.[52]

Amzi and Rose (Steele) Smith had nine other children besides Hank: Edith born in 1898 followed by Earl in1900, Elston in 1902, Nellie in 1905, Marvin in 1908, Richard in 1909, Ethel in 1910, Florence in 1914, and Elwood in 1921. The couple's first home was a two floor house built in an embankment behind the Pleasant Valley School. The house was very practical since, strategically hiding his upright still in the lower back room. Amzi was thus able to drive up the embankment to the rear upper floor of the house to unload cider and sugar for storage. From there, the ingredients could be easily poured through a hatch in the floor into the top of the upright still below. Although well suited for a secluded moonshine operation, there was little space for Amzi to grow his own apples. He thus later relocated down the Harmony Brass Castle Road, where he bought the property now known as Apgar's orchard and cider press. Although the business now carries the Apgar name it was Amzi who began it prior to Prohibition. An apple orchard and the cider it produced was the perfect cost reducing

---

51 *Easton Express/Easton Argus Harmony News* of 12 March and 16 April 1920.
52 The still story was provided by Dick Smith; that of Hank's sad subsequent life was provided by Emma (Simon) Raywood, Viola Cruts's sister.

complement to Amzi's already established applejack operation and the sale of apples gave him legitimacy. Dick Smith was quick to point out that "you can't make a living on just selling cider!" One of Amzi's granddaughters still clearly remembers her somewhat scary excitement when, as a small child, she ran after her older siblings who at times, on instructions of their grandfather, sped off down the slope behind their grandparents house through a grassy field to hide things in a fence row. Although she didn't know exactly what was happening, she knew it was a "big deal". [53]

Amzi's eldest son Earl who had been working with his father eventually took over the cider press and fruit orchard operation from his parents around 1924 before his marriage and owned/managed it during Prohibition. The decision to sell to Earl may have been due to a coasting accident on a sled in 1920 when Amzi ran into a tree and was severely injured.[54] Soon after this accident Amzi moved up a private lane off nearby Ridge Road, next to which Elwood and Hank were given land on which to build homes.

With Earl now in charge of the orchards, both cider and applejack production grew substantially but he couldn't run the operation on his own. A solution; however, was readily at hand. Since Earl Smith had married Rose Apgar of Mansfield Township and his younger sister Ethel Smith had married Rose's brother Ellis Martin Apgar on 3 July 1931 (brother and sister had married brother and sister), Earl and his wife urged their younger siblings to move to the farm where Ellis was hired by Earl to help manage the business and was rented half of Earl's house, across from the Cider press. Although the two couples had to share the same bathroom, it seemed like a perfect arrangement. In practice; however, problems arose. Before the arrival of Ellis and Ethel, Earl had already had a close call with the law. In 1924 he was in court regarding $1,000 he had given State Trooper Edward Kalber after Kalber found an empty still on his property which Earl intended to use in making applejack. Kalber was later arrested and charged with extortion in receiving the money but testified in his defense that the payment was not due to any threat, but was simply "a loan". When Earl however testified as to whether the money he gave Kalber was a loan he unhesitatingly replied, "I considered it gone". Kalber was subsequently con-

---

53 As recounted by Amzi's granddaughter, Rose (Smith) Kinney.
54 The sledding accident was reported by the *Easton Express/Easton Argus* on 20 February 1920 p8.

victed, sentenced to three years behind bars, thus bringing his career as a trooper to an abrupt end.[55]

After that brush with the law, Earl became more cautious about his operations and the arrival of Ellis and Ethel worked to his advantage since, whereas Earl loved his drink, Ellis and Ethel shunned alcohol. Earl thus conveniently asked his brother-in-law partner to be present at the business whenever the Revenuers came for inspections. It was thus, during one of these inspection visits when Earl was conveniently absent that his illicit moonshine operation was discovered, and in the absence of Earl, it was Ellis's name that became permanently recorded in the Revenue records. Ethel was furious at her brother when this happened and never forgave Earl even after he eventually died of alcoholism related problems in the late 1930s.

Although Earl's wife Rose retained ownership of the orchards/cider mill after Earl's death, ownership eventually passed to Ellis and Ethel (Smith) Apgar in 1951 and the business has since carried the Apgar name. Ellis passed away in 1986 at age 76 just after the couple's 55th wedding anniversary. His obituary indicated that he was a self employed farmer and operated the cider press for 55 years, thus, beginning in 1931 the year of his marriage to Ethel, two years before the end of Prohibition. Under his strict management, of course, only apples, peaches, and cider were produced. Ethel followed Ellis five years later on March 24th 1991. Both now lay at rest in the Montana Cemetery on the mountaintop up the same road from where they lived and worked. Ellis and Ethel were both self-avowed teetotalers. They not only scorned alcohol in all forms but felt equally strongly about smoking.

Alan, the only son of Ellis and Ethel (Smith) Apgar, born in 1937, assumed ownership of the Apgar orchards and Cider press in the early 1980s and managed its operations until he passed away on April 5th 2013. Despite his father's aversion to alcohol, he always remembered going with his father as a young boy to deliver applejack to customers around Lake Hopatcong during the time Ellis worked with his Uncle Earl.[56] If Alan ever learned the art of distilling his ancestors' famous brew, he never said so. On the passing of his parents, their basement was found to be filled with bottles of alcohol they had been given over the years for Christmas and other occasions which, as teetotalers, they

---

55 *Easton Express* article "State Trooper Convicted On Two Counts Gets Three Years" of February 23rd 1931 p1.
56 As remembered by Alan's grandson Kevin E. Gilmore

had never touched. Alan and his wife Joan were thus left to dispose of this unexpected cache. Their ranch home which sits just down the road opposite the family cider mill and fruit stand is where they raised their two girls Cindy Lou and Linda Sue.

Alan's sister Doris who married Richard McKeever lives opposite them a few hundred yards further down on part of the land that also once belonged to her grandfather Amzi. Her son Tim has a home next door. She also has two other sons, Glen and Jeff, and a daughter Wendy. Today the Orchards and cider press are run by Alan's wife Joan, her daughter Cindy and Doris's son Tim. Its fruit stand is a landmark very popular with local residents.

Apart from Earl, Ethel's second brother Marvin born in 1908, may also have had a bootleg whiskey operation just up the stream from his father and brother Earl. Bruce Unangst remembers meeting Marvin's brother Earl, who told him that Marvin used to "work across the street" from the Unangst home which is nothing but woods with the Lopatcong Creek going through. Dick Smith had already told me that area had a number of well hidden stills in that area which lay just below his house. Marvin had been married twice and his second wife Emmy took all that he had. [57]

---

[57] Information on Marvin Smith was provided by Bruce Unangst and Doris McKeever.

Chapter Ten

THE BELVIEW "CHICKEN OPERATION"

Not all clandestine bootlegging operations were on the mountain top. At the base of Montana Mountain where the Lommason Glen road meets the Belvidere Road and across from where the Dairy Queen (now Zeek's Place) was built, stands a farmstead next to the Bel Pike Lanes Bowling Alley. The farm is currently operated by the Smith's (not related to Walt and Harry) and before them it was owned by the Gauls, but in the late 1920s/early 30s it was run by some city folks who once lived in the New York City area but later ran a large chicken raising operation from this farm. A neighbor at that time, Mary (Wieghorst) Warden, who lived with her parents and sister Jane on the first farm on Lommason Glen road and whose father once farmed the triangular field on which the Dairy Queen was later to sit remembers from her childhood that the chicken houses sat in plain sight parallel to the road and that shipments of crated live chickens were routinely sent to the insatiable New York market, almost on a weekly basis. Another neighbor who would have observed this activity was Henry Dinger, the long time principle of Harmony Township School, whose first home after marriage was the old Lommason Glen schoolhouse located across from the Wieghorsts. Every day farm laborers and neighbors around the farm would get whiffs of what seemed like bread baking. It was a pleasant smell, a smell of yeast, not so unusual for a farm in those days, and therefore it didn't raise any eyebrows.[58] The trucks regularly leaving the chicken farm were somewhat odd however; since whether the crates were filled with chickens or entirely empty, you couldn't see through them to the other side. The

---

58 Note: Cloth soaked in wet bread dough was used by moonshiners to seal joints in a still. When the still is fired up a very pleasant aroma of oven baked bread is produced.

toll takers and police on the New Jersey/New York bridges eventually found this odd as well and word must have gotten around.

Then one day there was a commotion at the farm and word spread like wildfire across the mountain. Federal Agents had arrived and were breaking up a still! The truck that had made so many chicken runs to New York was now also searched and found to have a secret compartment in the middle of all the crates. Now it was clear why no one could see through the chicken crates to the other side. Something was blocking the view and it turned out it was an inner room filled with kegs of whiskey! The operation had eluded detection by all eyes for a number of years but now the secret was out, disaster had struck, and the operation had come to an abrupt end. Coincidentally, the day before the raid there was an advertisement in the newspaper regarding a calf for sale at that farm and Mary's father, responding to the ad, went to look at the calf the next day. On his arrival at the farm he was met by the Feds who gave him the 3rd degree asking questions about who he was, why he was there, and what his relationship to the chicken vendors was. Fortunately for him, he was able to pull out the Easton Express article regarding the calf for sale to explain his presence! [59] As "city people", this family, like that of Rufus Smith, was considered by the mountain bootlegging folk as "outsiders". Unlike Rufus however, they were never welcomed into the fold by the local born mountain bootleggers.

From back up on the mountain, Dick's assertion that "in the old days of Prohibition on this mountain everyone was a bootlegger; everyone was involved in making moonshine" rang in my ears whenever I was given a tip on someone else I needed to talk to, and although I found that the majority of the actors lived on the mountain, they clearly were not alone.[60]

---

59 Story provided by Mary (Wieghorst) Warden. A deed search revealed that from April 1928, this property was owned by a couple named Alfred F. and Leslie Lanterman.
60 The Emery family who lived less than a mile up Lommason Glen across from the Chicken operation was involved in Bootlegging as well since the *Phillipsburg Star* reported in an article 'Troopers Arrest Two Bootleggers at Butzville" of 30 July 1931 that Harry Emery and Daniel Kane both of Montana were captured with three gallons of barley whiskey for which they were arraigned and released under a $500 bond each awaiting action by the Grand Jury. Again in December that year Emery was arrested for unlawful transportation of liquor but received a suspended sentence as he had a wife with seven children. Ref: *The Phillipsburg Star* article "Liquor Cases Net County $1200 in Fines" of 17 December 1931 p1.

Chapter Eleven
THE LOCAL BOOTLEGGER OUTLET SURFACES IN NEARBY PHILLIPSBURG

NYC Deputy Police Commissioner John A. Leach, right, watching agents pour liquor into a sewer after a Prohibition raid (such scenes were common in Phillipsburg, NJ during Prohibition with the precious liquid flowing through sewers straight to the Delaware River). [61]

Although the Smiths, Steeles, Denkers, and Bob Clower had multiple outlets for their prized bootleg (some as far away as Newark and New York) and people in the know would line up at their door, there were also some local supply hungry "speakeasy" bars that operated during Prohibition in nearby communities of Brainards, Belvidere, New Village, and Oxford. The town of Phillipsburg was, in fact, full of

---

61 Source: *New York World-Telegram* and the *Sun Newspaper* Photograph Collection/Library of Congress, Washington, D.C. (neg. no. LC-USZ62-123257).

them and gambling- using dice, punch boards, and slot machines-was common.[62] A Phillipsburg tavern owner in recent times told me that when he renovated his building to update its facilities he found pipes in the partitions coming from an upstairs room to the ground floor that were not water pipes. He also found cash stuffed behind some of the walls National Currency notes, in circulation during Prohibition, which had town names printed on them. Unfortunately, this fortuitous discovery had already been made by rats & mice which over the years had made good use of most of the stash by shredding it for their nests.

The taverns that remained operational during Prohibition did so at great risk since heavy fines and imprisonment were regularly imposed on those unfortunate enough to be caught. The highest level of discretion was thus maintained between buyer and seller for business to run smoothly, making it difficult today to know who was supplying who. As Warren County Prosecutor Sylvester Smith admitted during Prohibition, it was difficult to find detectives to work undercover to trap/apprehend violators since these officers would have to drink side by side with the violators and in the event of an arrest of a pal, the confederates would find and "get" the rat.[63]

On May 22, 2015, however, the Warren Reporter newspaper printed an article celebrating the 100th Anniversary of Steve's Café at 766 South Main Street in Phillipsburg, which was purchased by Steve Ignatz in 1915 for $3,500 when it was known as "The Morris House" (the Morris Canal passed by the back door). This Steve (Jr.) immigrated to the US as a young man from Hungary in 1900 with his father and two siblings. He met his wife, Ethel Gaydo, at a cigar factory in Passaic NJ where she worked and he frequented to buy cigars for his first bar in Franklin, NJ. The article stated that Phillipsburg once boasted 54 taverns and that the current proprietor's grandfather "would pick up booze from Montana Mountain and Allentown" and that he would get it by car wherein "the seat had a false bottom and

---

62 Other Lehigh Valley towns were equally notorious including Easton, known then as "The Little Apple", to where many patrons would make week-end trips to enjoy illegal booze, gambling and professional female company (Ref: *Easton PA: Special Projects*, Richard F. Hope, Lulu Press 2013 pp169,170) and Bethlehem PA where people like social critic H.L. Mencken and his publisher Alfred Knopf could enjoy a Bach choir performance followed by a visit to an establishment with a signboard marked "Sea food" to enjoy a few "Humpen" steins of beer before catching a train back to New York City. (Ref: Adam T. Bentz, *Raids and Responsibility : Prohibition Enforcement and Evasion in the 1920s Lehigh Valley and the Unlikely Administration of Bethlehem Reform Mayor Robert Pfeifle* p31).

63 See *The Washington Star* article "Bootleggers Hard to Trap" of April 3rd 1924 p1.

he would sit granny and three kids on it". I thought there could only be a few possible suppliers for this booze, and my prime suspects were the Smith brothers, or the notorious Bob Clower since others seemed to prefer direct shipments to Newark/New York. I therefore sought out the current proprietor for a confirmation. Maryann Ignatz, great-granddaughter of the first owner, confirmed what I had already suspected, she never heard the suppliers' names.
The secret was thus well kept.

The Morris House had a fascinating history as a Speakeasy during Prohibition (Its name did not change to "Steve's Café until 1939). When his father died in 1921 at the start of Prohibition, Steve Jr., proprietor of the Morris House, was 38 years of age. Maryann's Aunt Elsie (Steve Jr.'s daughter) often told her that she had a baby carriage as a child and that her father would send her around the neighborhood with her baby doll and a bottle companion tucked nicely under the covers. She was instructed to push her carriage to one of her father's friends' houses which would be flagged by a red cloth on the porch or clothes line for easy identification. When she arrived the customer would take out the baby's big bottle and tuck some money in its place to take back to her father. Elsie also remembered her father waking her in the middle of the night "to go for a ride to Allentown" telling her that "if anyone stops us on the way you should tell them you are sick and I'm taking you to the doctor's". Elsie and Steve III would also often repeat the story of the police officer who got drunk in their father's Speakeasy and was taken to their living room next door to sleep it off. Suddenly waking up, his first words were "who stole my whiskey bottle?!"

Steve Jr. became a busy man during Prohibition. Maryann herself remembers her own father (Steve III), taking her and her mother on Sunday rides to show them where, in 1929 at age 17, he was sent to pick up liquor in Allentown/Bethlehem for his father, and where the drop-off points were on the return trip through Freemansburg, Glendon, and the Huffs' store in Warren Glen.[64] Her Dad would laugh about that time, referring to himself as "a teenage Rum Runner"! The raids by Federal and local Prohibition Enforcement Officers in Phil-

---

[64] Joseph Huff later moved with his family to 686 S. Main St. Phillipsburg where he continued his grocery business. On Sept. 11th 1925 he was raided & arrested after two containers of whiskey were found. (ref: *Easton Express* article of Sept 12th 1925 *Huff arrested, Furnished Bail for Court*).

lipsburg were frequent and caused the family a great deal of anguish. They believe, in fact, that the early death of Steve Jr.'s wife, Ethel (Gaydo) Ignatz, in December 1928 at age 37 from a burst ulcer was due to the stress she suffered from those raids when even the mattresses on their beds were torn open.[65] The family felt that neighbors, jealous of the new cars they saw next door, were the informers responsible for this raid. The profits were indeed significant and conspicuous consumption ensued. "Grandpop" Steve Ignatz not only owned many homes in Alpha but also about half of the town's acreage and gave his son Steve III the honor of naming three of the town's streets which were dubbed Morris, Warren, and Harding. Steve Jr. also had a home in Winter Haven, Florida a summer home in Carpentersville, a farm in Asbury, and multiple properties in Phillipsburg including a gas station on South Main Street. Not bad for someone who was listed in the 1930 census as a real estate agent operating from his office home at 768 South Main Street! Despite these assets, Steve Jr. felt personal guilt in the premature death of his wife and his health deteriorated. Focusing on his son, in 1930, as a graduation present, he sailed with Steve III on the luxurious S.S. Mauretania for a three-month tour of Europe visiting Hungary, Czechoslovakia, France, and Italy and while there, they got treatment in the sulfur springs of Budapest and later had an audience with Pope Pius XI and got to kiss his ring. [66]

After their return home, however, Steve's despondency over the loss of his wife returned and he began gambling as a hobby, playing cards at the Elks, often losing heavily. His legacy during this period in the midst of the Great Depression is however not his wealth or extravagances, but his philanthropy. This people remember with overwhelming gratitude to this day. He helped finance the building of area churches in Alpha and Phillipsburg such as St. Peter's and St. Paul's on South Main Street, Phillipsburg, donated to schools and hospitals, financed Elks Club food baskets, and allowed tenants in his properties to live rent free during the Great Depression when they had lost their jobs/

---

65 One such raid at the Ignatz residence was reported on June 12th 1926 p8 by the *Easton Express* as one of three places "visited" by local police, the others being those of J.P. Smith and Louis Kish. Ref Article "Police Visit Three Saloons But They Failed to Find Liquor at Either Place".

66 Interestingly, on the return trip, two days off Le Havre Steve III placed a postcard in a bottle and threw it off the deck of the S/S Mauretania. Forty-Two years later, the bottle washed up on the shore in Jones Beach NY. (Ref: *Easton Express* article "Forty-Two Year Sea Traveller Lands" of 18 Mar 1972 by Jim Shelly p8.).

incomes and were unable to pay. He also provided solace, in the form of whiskey, the source of his wealth, to mourners during wakes and contributed to charities to help the poor. Steve III (who ran the Café from 1939) was an accomplished musician who played violin, piano, and banjo with his group "Steve and His Night Owls". His daughter Maryann now carries the torch.

That is the story of one Phillipsburg Speakeasy. The town was in fact peppered with them, some of which had slot machines, and the raids would receive regular coverage in the local press. Montana Mountain was in fact surrounded by such outlets in the nearby communities of Brainards, Belvidere, New Village, and Washington. Les Kober clearly remembers that when his father's own stock went low he would go down to Rossini's Meat Market in New Village and ask for "a bottle". If there was hesitation behind the counter Gabe would say "No bottle, no Meat!" During a raid on the county seat at Belvidere in 1926, the owner of a candy store, a barber and three private homes were raided. At the barber shop, liquor was being dispensed from a bottle and a bonafide bootlegger was generally available with a flask in his hip pocket![67]

Phillipsburg was a beehive of activity during Prohibition and Steve Ignatz is only one example of those who followed the "Carpe Diem" philosophy. Maryann Ignatz told me that in the 1970s/80s the Guinness Book of World Records listed the town as sharing, along with Hoboken NJ, the honor of having most bars per square mile of any towns in the US. Going through records of the period, I found that prior to Prohibition Phillipsburg had 35 establishments where alcohol could be served (10 bars/restaurants and 25 hotels) of which most were shut down during Prohibition (there were only 5 hotels listed in 1930!).[68] Many, however, continued business throughout the period as "Speakeasies" or operated from private residences. Federal Prohibition Enforcement officer Fred Kroesen, who had moved his residence to Phillipsburg seemed to have been everywhere on a raiding frenzy with his team. There were also sensational heists. On April 12th 1924, for example, the Easton Express reported that after a "Mr. O'Neill" failed

---

67 Ref: *The Washington Star* newspaper article "Booze Raid at Belvidere" of 7 May 1937. The arrestees were Kline Hess, owner of the candy store, Fletcher Blazier, the barber along with Fannie and Roy Smith. The candy store owner was also charged with gambling on his premises.
68 Source for establishment numbers: West's Easton PA and Phillipsburg NJ Directories for 1928 & 1930.

to pick up a rail cargo of "Fish-Perishable" Kroesen investigated and found the car filled with 150 half barrels of illicit lager and ordered it seized and shipped to Federal warehouses in Newark. After giving the instructions, Kroesen left. A short while later, at the moment the car was moved to another track, two men appeared with two large trucks announcing they were dry agents sent to take possession of the cargo and the goods were quickly loaded and dispatched. Soon after their departure, legitimate dry agents arrived and were aghast to find the cargo gone. The culprits were never apprehended.[69]

Rail was a favorite medium of transport. On July 27th 1931 four freight cars transiting through Phillipsburg labeled "scrap brass" were found to be loaded with high powered beer and were thus re-routed to the Federal authorities in Newark.[70] On August 30th 1929 in what was known as the Pursel Street Raid, 30 half barrels and 12 full barrels of beer were seized the old Washington Extract Plant and destroyed by pouring the contents into the street and sewers. At exciting occasions such as these police would not intervene when neighbors and onlookers would gather around and scoop up some of the precious contents as it flowed through the gutters![71] Violence was not uncommon as was demonstrated when, in 1932, Louis Kuklis murdered Alex Cojenski with a pick handle in an argument over a still Kuklish was operating.[72] A chronology of events involving Phillipsburg violators of the previsions of the Volstead Act is provided in annex 3.

Phillipsburg men also exported their skills. When a 1500 gallon still was seized by the Federal Enforcement Agents in Newark in March 1931 along with seven huge vats of mash seven feet wide and twelve feet deep, the only person on the premises was the presumed owner, a well dressed young man who gave his name as Chris Piazza of Phillipsburg. Piazza was arrested against $1,500 bail which was readily

---

69 Ref *Easton Express* article "Beer Shipped from Phillipsburg Carried Away By Fake Dry Agents" of 12 April 1924 p8.
70 *Easton Express* article "Seize Four Cars of Beer" of 27 July 27 1931.
71 Easton Express article "Federal Men Conduct Raid" of August 31st 1929 p8. Similarly, back in 1922 in nearby Easton, after 60 gallons of liquor taken from a bar ironically also named "Steve's Café" was poured into the gutter many in the crowd of onlookers "hurried to the scene carrying Dixie drinking cups and other utensils with which to slake their thirsts" (*Easton Daily Free Press* of 24 August 1922).
72 Ref *The Phillipsburg Star* article "Phillipsburg Man Indicted for Murder" of 29 September 1932 p1.

paid.[73] Pocket change…

Phillipsburg was also the turf of Walt's Smith's close friend Joe McDermott who had one foot in his Harmony Oakhurst Café and the other at his Phillipsburg Club House Café. Joe was well known by the local police and judges. On December 31st 1924 he was arrested during a raid for illegal possession of intoxicating liquors and provided $1,000 bail. About a month later he was again arrested for the same offense and provided another $1,000 bail but at the trial got away with only a $550 fine and a thirty-day jail sentence, which was suspended on "the condition of his good behavior."[74] On November 29th 1927 Joe was again in court, when he and Constable Chris Rehfuss (one of the officials who raided and shot at Bob Clower, the "Low's Hollow Desperado" three years earlier) were charged with conspiracy with regard to the seizure of 20 half barrels of beer from a warehouse. The case ended in a mistrial.[75] Joe's brother John was also well known to local police having been arrested for driving a truck with fictitious license plates which contained 33 half barrels of beer.[76] Despite all this activity and outcries against it by temperance groups, some New Jersey State politicians remained in denial. The office of one, in fact, reported in 1929 that Warren and Hunterdon counties "are the only real bone dry counties in the state" and that "there had been no complaints for five years".[77]

By 1930 the pendulum had begun to swing toward repeal of the 18th Amendment. In that year Warren County contributed to the election of Dwight W. Morrow as a US Senator for New Jersey. Morrow had been a partner in the Morgan banking house, Ambassador to Mexico, and was the father-in-law of Charles Lindbergh, but more importantly was one of the foremost advocates of the repeal of Prohibition. Although he died suddenly of a cerebral hemorrhage the follow-

---

73 *Easton Express* article "Big Still Seized by Federal Agents One Man Giving Phillipsburg as His Home Was Placed Under Arrest" of 5 Mar 1931 p8. .
74 *Easton Express* articles "State Troopers Conducted Another Raid in Phillipsburg" of 1 January 1925, "End of Week of Liquor Trials in The Warren County Court" of 6 February 1925, & "Kowolick and McDermott Last to Face the Court, Fined but Escape Terms in Prison" of 28 May 1925.
75 Easton Express articles "Conspiracy Charge Against Phillipsburgers Continued" of 21 November 1927, "Rehfuss and McDermott Face Charge of Conspiracy in Beer Case" of 24 November 1927, "Hint At Jury Tampering Brings Beer Trial to a Sudden End" of 29 November 1927, and Beer Trial Comes to a Sudden End of 1 December 1927.
76 Ibid. article "Beer Truck Had Wrong Plates" of 14 July 1931.
77 The Congressman referred to was Charles A. Eaton of North Plainfield. Ref. *Easton Express* article "Warren and Hunterdon Only Dry Counties in New Jersey" of 20 June 1929.

ing October, New Jersey stood firm. A statistical booklet published by the "Association Against the 18th Amendment" in 1930 indicated that although there were 50,000 prohibition prisoners in jail, 88 percent of violators were not jailed as felons. Prohibition cases represented two-thirds of cases tried Federal Courts and 18-20,000 cases were pending. The cost of adequate Prohibition Enforcement was estimated at $100 million/year and $350 million with jury hearings.[78] In the meantime, profits remained high and while stills were regularly destroyed, others sprouted up like mushrooms. It should be noted that, though operating stills of up to 1,000 gallon capacity, the Montana Mountain folk were small players in the big game even as compared with other parts of the state. On July 18th 1930, for example, the local press reported that a 7,500 gallon still had be seized in Patterson, NJ along with 2,000 gallons of whiskey and 50,000 gallons of mash valued at $100,000,[79] and even that was dwarfed by a 25,000 gallon still seized at nearby Island Park in Easton, Pennsylvania.[80] The market seemed insatiable. In what must have seemed the epitome of hypocrisy, the planting of an undercover agent in the US Senate with the full cooperation of Vice President Curtis led to the arrest and conviction of George Cassiday, known as the "Man in the Green Hat", who had been operating there continuously from 1920-29, doing a booming business with Senators and Congressmen. The names of the honorable clients listed in Cassiday's customer book were however carefully withheld by the Prohibition Bureau and the Department of Justice.[81]

The momentum toward repeal of the 18th Amendment continued. In September 1931 the American Bar Association came out publicly in favor of it and on January 5th 1932 repeal of the New Jersey's Prohibition Enforcement Act failed by only two votes. The Warren County Federation for Temperance and Law Observance help ensure its failure by presenting a petition of about 700 signatures to Sen. Theodore Dawes requesting him to vote against the repeal of this statute also called the Hobart State Enforcement Act. Still, the Democrats won a clean sweep in the Warren County elections that year and a Democrat, Harry Moore was elected Governor. By this time, (July 1931) the force

---

78 *Easton Express* article "Places Blame on Dry Law" of 26 December 1930.
79 Ibid. article "$100,000 Liquor Plant is Seized in Paterson" of 18 July 1930.
80 Ibid. article "25,000 Gallon Alcohol Plant Raided Near Island Park" of 20 October 1932
81 In more recent times, a similar scandal arose surrounding Deborah Jane Palfrey, the "D.C. Madame", whose client list from 1993-2006 was never released although a number of high level government officials resigned "for personal reasons".

of Federal Dry agents had reached 1,900 nationwide.

That January, in a sobering analogy which has special relevance today, Yandell Henderson, Professor of Applied Physiology at Yale University and member of the National Academy of Sciences, testified before Congress that beer containing from three to four percent alcohol was not intoxicating and actually had social advantages. He declared that "beer drinking hurts no one while football the other great student amusement, killed forty young men and boys this past season".[82] The President of the American Dental Association also testified that beer and light wines were advocated for the nutrition of expecting mothers and development of unborn child's teeth.[83] In June of that year J. D. Rockefeller Jr. stated that, in his opinion, Prohibition had failed and in the Democratic National Convention that month it was said that the sudden rise of anti-prohibition sentiment there "had been one of dramatic episodes of political history" surprising delegates "as much as if the waters of Lake Michigan had risen into their hotels."[84]

Despite this visible change in sentiment, New Jersey remained firm in Prohibition enforcement leading the Third Prohibition district (Pennsylvania, New Jersey and Delaware) during the fiscal year ending on June 30th 1931 with over 6 million gallons of illegal alcohol seized, more than 66 percent of the total for all three states. The capacity of the 409 stills seized was 626,567 gallons out of a district total of about 726,000 gallons.[85] New Jersey continued to lead the district in February of 1932 year with 16 large distilleries raided, 239 seizures resulting in 283 arrests and 55 stills and 38 automobiles seized 173 convictions, 200 jail sentences and 73 fines.[86]

Incredibly, one Federal Judge in New Jersey estimated that the Eighteenth Amendment was violated 75 million times a year in the

---

82 Ibid. article "Yale Professor Defends Beer" of 8 January 1932. (my italics as the issue remains relevant to this day). A Washington Star article "Lafayette's Liquor Bill" of May 6th 1926 criticized the affect of the Volstead Act on student life at Lafayette College in Easton PA. claiming $50,000 was spent annually by students and that "The students of Lafayette College are and will continue to be a legitimate prey for bootleggers as long as..the Volstead Act continues to exist".
83 Ibid. article "Beer Foe of Malnutrition Dr. Martin Dewey Testifies" of 20 January 1932.
84 Ibid. article "Prohibition Overshadows other Policies at Gathering" of 14 June 1932.
85 Ibid. article "Much Liquor found in State" of 28 August 1931.
86 Ibid. article "New Jersey Leads in Liquor Seizures" of 18 March 1932.

state![87] Norman Schwarzkopf Sr., appointed by Governor Edwards as first superintendent of the NJ State Police in 1921 (and father of present day's "Stormin Norman") had his hands full, partly since corruption within the police force was rampant. (In one case, six of his troopers had to be dismissed for accepting bribes for protecting beer trucks).[88]

In September 1932 the American Legion then overwhelmingly demanded repeal and wrote to President Hoover to press the issue. Two months later, on December 5th a resolution proposing a constitutional amendment to repeal the 18th Amendment was introduced in Congress. With the election of FDR in 1932, the end was near. Within weeks after he took office in March 1933, in the midst of the Great Depression, he signed the Beer and Wine Revenue Act which redefined intoxicating liquors under the Volstead Act, thus legalizing 3.2% alcohol while levying a federal tax on it to raise much need revenue for his "New Deal" recovery programs. The Feds then focused exclusively on illegal liquor manufacture and transport, leaving speakeasy prosecution to the states. From that point on the New Jersey press seemed to be focused more on Sunday drinking laws and illegal slot machines than Prohibition enforcement.[89] In July 1933 the local press reported only twelve prisoners in the county jail, said to be only half the usual number of previous years and blamed the eighteenth amendment for creating criminals and filling prisons. Times were changing...[90]

---

87 As estimated by Judge George M. Bourquin of Trenton (Judge Bourquin of Montana State, called to NJ to help clean up a congested criminal calendar); ref *Easton Express* article "75 Million Dry Violations" of 1 October 1931. Considering the huge volume, this judge encouraged defendants to plead guilty. He once disposed of the pleas of forty defendants in four minutes!

88 *Easton Express* article "New Jersey discharges Six Cops for Taking Bribes" of 4 October 1931.

89 Phillipsburg's Sunday liquor law was adopted in December 1949. Ref *Easton Express* Article "Sunday Liquor Law is Adopted In Phillipsburg" of 8 December 1949. Harmony followed soon after in November 1950 following a petition of over 160 signatures submitted to the Township Committee by John Drenscho, owner of the Buckhorn Casino. Ref *Easton Express* article "Harmony to Vote on Sunday Sales of Liquor Nov 7" of 11 September 1950.

90 *The Phillipsburg Star* article "Few Prisoners In County Jail Report to Board" of 7 July 1933.

The Ignatz's: Steve I, Steve II, Steve III.

Maryann Stephanie Ignatz daughter of Steve III and current owner/operator of Steve's Cafe.

Interior of Steve's Cafe/Morris House.

Chapter Twelve
OLD TIMES DIE HARD: AFTER THE FALL

Finally, on December 5th 1933 Prohibition was repealed with the passage of the 21st Amendment to the Constitution. An era had ended and the light at the end of the dark tunnel had been reached. Unfortunately, former Governor (and later Senator) Edwards, "one of the wettest of the wets" didn't live to see the jubilation it produced having died in 1931 ill and despondent from a self-inflicted gunshot wound after losing his wife in 1928, and his fortune during the stock market crash the following year. Although a Prohibition Party existed in New Jersey after Repeal popular support for it was virtually non-existent. Its gubernatorial candidate in the 1937 election, Eugene A. Smith, received only 15 votes in Warren County compared with 8,008 for the Democratic candidate Harry Moore who eventually won the election.[91] Prohibition was officially dead. In its place were millions of dollars in Federal tax revenue. In 1934 New Jersey contributed about $15 million in liquor fiscal taxes of which $13.3 million were generated from the fifth district comprising the eleven northern counties including Warren.[92] The State of New Jersey was also on the gravy train reaping significant revenues. Receipts from liquor licenses from January-December 1936 amounted to over $4.2 million. During this period Warren County reaped $36,400 from the issuance 133 plenary consumption licenses, another $1,400 from retail distribution licenses

---

[91] The Prohibition Gubernatorial candidate for NJ was Eugene A. Smith. For the 1937 election results see *Easton Express* article "Official Vote in Warren County" of 8 November 1937 p8.
[92] Ref: *Easton Express* article "Millions in Liquor Taxes" of 14 January 1935 p.8. Pennsylvania was #1 with $54.2 million followed by New York with $52.2 million and Illinois with $50.7 million.

and another $1,900 in club licensing fees.[93] One enterprising individual even requested a license to peddle beer in NJ along roads like ice cream from an ice cream truck! The petitioner was informed by the State Beverage Commission that while the idea was conceived in good faith "it would not be received in good humor". A patent proposal for "liquorized ice cream" fused with such liquors as rum, cognac, whiskey and scotch suffered a similar fate.[94] By the end of 1940, seven years after repeal, receipts from liquor taxes in the eleven northern NJ counties totaled $160.3 million[95] Impressive? Yes, but bootleggers still thrived, and stills proliferated when the Federal fiscal tax on alcohol was raised in 1941. Already in 1935 a man named Robert J. Burns was arrested on Montana Mountain and charged with possession of an unlicensed and untaxed still and he furnished $2,000 bail awaiting trial.[96] In a 1941 news article entitled "Bootleggers are Back in New Jersey" Alfred Deiscoll head of the NJ ABC (Alcoholic Beverage Commission) that year expressed his frustration saying "illicit whiskey only costs about five cents a quart to make and the margin of profit in the sale of the product attracts many misguided individuals".[97] Bootleggers in fact had not come back, they had never left! In fact, during the 1945/46 fiscal year 151 out of 196 liquor related arrests were for bootlegging[98] and while local taverns in Harmony and nearby towns quickly resumed public sales of the now legalized (and taxed) alcoholic beverages, untaxed bootleg whiskey was often available under-the-table in some watering holes. Dick Smith thus remembers that during WWII and thereafter some local bartenders, like John Drenchko at the Buck-

---

93 It should be noted however that along with significant state revenue came a spate in drunken driving charges. Driver License revocations rose from 1,305 in 1935 to 1,534 in 1936 (a 17.5% increase); ref Easton Express article "Motor License Revocations show Big Increase in 1936" of 19 January 1937 p8. In 1938 drunken driving arrests were greatly facilitated by the first alcohol breath test developed by Dr. R.N. Harger aptly named the "Drunkometer". Blood tests were not introduced until 1945. (ref *Easton Express* article of 25 June 1945 p8 "Don't Argue When Blood Tests Show Man Drunk, Medical Journal Says").
94 Ref: *Easton Express* article "Peddling Beer Meets Disfavor" of 14 June 1941 p8 (my italics); ref liqourized ice cream see *The Phillipsburger* newspaper article "No Liquor Ice Cream for Jersey" of July 14th, 1938.
95 Ibid. article "$477,217 Paid in Six Months for State Beverage Licenses; Dr Burnett Reports 9448 Plenary Retail Consumption and 1396 Plenary Retail Distribution Permits" of 15 January 1937 p8. Ref the 1940 figure. See *Easton Express* article "Millions Paid in Liquor Taxes" of 13 December 1940 p8.
96 Ref: *Easton Express* article "Man Arrested in Still Raid in Warren County" of 4 June 1935 p8.
97 Ibid. article "Bootleggers are Back in New Jersey" of 27 November 1941 p8. *(my italics).*
98 Ibid. article "Jersey ABC Agents Nab 151 Bootleggers" of 25 July 1946 p8.

horn Casino on Belvidere road, would discretely serve homemade corn whiskey or applejack. The situation remained the same in 1949 when then Governor Driscoll said "High Federal taxes constitute an open invitation for illicit operators to set up business".[99] Little action was taken even by 1951 when a $3/gallon excise tax increase was proposed whereas bootleg whiskey could then be produced and delivered to the consumer for $1 or less![100]

To the Smith brothers Walt, Harry, and Clarence of Harmony, repeal meant little and business continued as usual. There were hiccups however, as it seems to have taken them a while to accept the fact that, to be legal, their operations now required affixing fiscal tax labels on their product. Walt was the first to learn this hard lesson when, in January 1937, he paid $1,000 bail after being arrested and charged with possession of two barrels of unstamped liquor which were duly confiscated.[101] Harry's turn came in July the following year when he and his wife Dorothy were both charged- he with one count of possession and one of sale of liquor, and his wife with sale. They both pleaded non vult, resulting in fines for each ($200 for himself and $100 for his wife.[102] Despite these risks, the New Jersey market appeared insatiable. By 1946, it in fact led the nation in per capita alcohol consumption[103]

Eventually the Smith brothers' distillery operations were transferred to a white brick building that the brothers built just up the road from Walt's house where production and sales went on legally and smoothly. Walt marketed his famous applejack under the name "Still No. 1". Clarence labeled his "Old Orchard Applejack" and "Warren Rye Whiskey" which were sold for $1.00 and 75 cents/quart respectively through "Kerns Quality Liquor Store" in nearby Phillipsburg. The building which housed the Smith Brothers' Distillery stands to this day. Dick Denker who lived upstairs in this distillery building in the mid-fifties after his marriage remembers Walt's unmistakable yodeling coming from his house up the road and echoing through the mountain valley almost every night.

---

99 Ibid. article "High U.S. Taxes Spurs Bootlegging Driscoll Declares" of 29 September 1949 p8.
100 Ibid. article "Bootlegger Rise Blamed on Higher Federal Levies" of 26 February 1951 p8.
101 Ibid article "Seized in Raid" of 9 January 1937 p. 8.
102 Ibid article "Fines are Imposed in Special Sessions" of 27 July 1938 p. 8.
103 Ibid article "Jersey Liquor Drinking Leads Entire Nation" of 31 October 1946 p.8.

The debate over Sunday alcohol sales-1949
(Source: Easton Express of 4 November 1949)

Humorous stories of Walt escapades continued on after Prohibition ended and many stories continue to circulate. One night, for example, Dick told me that after a boisterous evening at the Roxburg

Hotel soon known as the Lanark Inn, Walt said goodnight to his friends, including Dick, and went out to his car. Soon he was heard shouting from the parking lot, "Somebody stole my steering wheel! Somebody stole my steering wheel!" and his friends ran out to his aid. When they got to his car, there was Walt, sitting in the back seat instead of the front seat! [104] On March 16th 1947, Walt drove his car through a guard fence and came to a stop beside the tracks of the Lehigh and Hudson Railroad in Belvidere, where he was discovered by a train crew at four AM. In that incident he got off lightly being fined only five dollars and costs on a charge of careless driving.[105]

Then there was the story of Walt's bumpy landing when travelling past Alpha with his wife driving the car after he had lost his license. Nearing another of his favorite haunts, Walt asked Rosa to drop him off but she prudently refused. Walt thus simply opened the door, jumped out, rolled down the side of the road, got up and limped into the bar leaving his beloved Rosa in a state of desperation. [106]

Walt was great company to be with, whatever the circumstances. During one of his arrests Dick remembered going along with Walt's brother Harry to visit Walt at the county jail in Belvidere. Dick still laughs when he tells the story. Expecting to find Walt despondent, they instead on entering found him behind the bars in the midst of what appeared to be a lunch party with other inmates along with the female warden, who had gone into the cell to join the fun.[107]

On his release his was once again a frequent visitor at the Oakhurst in Hutchison. Although he was always welcome, he would at times both save money and show his generosity by bringing some of his own home brewed applejack along with him. Joe would explode when he caught him in the act saying "you S.O.B., you should be

---

104 Source of story: Dick Smith.
105 *Easton Express* article "Drivers fined in 2 Belvidere Accidents" of 17 Mar 1947 p8.
106 Story as recounted by Dick Smith.
107 A short term in the Warren County prison was not necessarily unpleasant. Already on April 21st 1933 *The Phillipsburg Star* was soliciting the public to donate a piano to make prisoner confinement "less irksome, their life much happier, the long and lonesome hours made to pass away more rapidly" (ref article "Piano wanted for Jail Inmates"). An *Easton Express* article "Warren Grand Jury Commends County Prison" of 11 January 1945 p8 later quoted the County Prosecutor as saying "compared to other jails he has seen, this one is a palace". A month later, in an article "State Inspector Lauds Condition Of County Jail" of February 23rd 1945 NJ inspectors considered the jail to be "a model of cleanliness" praising the warden Augustus Herbert and his wife (who did the cooking for the inmates). Augustus Herbert served as warden from 1945-1961.

drinking my drinks!!"

In another incident, Walt had lost his prized fox hound and was told by some people that they thought they saw it around Flannery's Tavern, near Belvidere. Dick Smith remembers that he and Walt went looking for the dog but stopped first at the tavern to make enquiries about whether it had been seen. After a number of drinks Walt suddenly fell backwards on his bar stool and knocked down most of the chairs and a table, ending up on the floor. Helen Flannery knew Walt very well, therefore, all was forgiven. They never did find the dog though.

Flannery's Tavern off Route 46 in the 1940s.

At one point in the '50s Harry became ill and thought he might have cancer. His wife Dorothy took him for a checkup at Warren Hospital. He wouldn't stay for the checkup though and returned to the car saying he wanted to return home. Occasionally friends and family would gather at Walt's house. On the 19th of March 1959, at one such gathering Harry was overheard saying as he left that he wanted to kill himself. Those who heard him passed it off as it wasn't the first time Harry talked about suicide. His words were thus not taken seriously, but later that afternoon when the Emergency Squad siren blared through the valley, reality struck like a bolt of lightning. Harry meant what he said. Apparently despondent over his ill health which kept him from working for the past few years, Harry had shot himself. The rescuers came, but there was nothing to do, the deed was done. Harry was gone leaving his family and friends devastated by the loss.

Walt continued the business with Clarence and his generosity was well known to all who knew him. Bob Vannatta, one-time Mayor of

Harmony, remembered walking in the woods one day with a friend when Walt came up to them and said, "Hey Bob wait here, I've got something for you" and soon returned with a bottle of his famous applejack for them. The mailman, Bobbie Young who lived over on the Harmony Brass Castle Road near the Apgars' also regularly received a thank you bottle for every holiday.[108]

Walt outlived Harry by 13 years, passing away on April 19th 1972, leaving Clarence who by this time had no desire to continue the family business and is reported to have sold the secret Smith Brothers recipe to Laird's Distillery of Scobeyville, New Jersey,[109] which still markets it today under the name of "Laird's Applejack". The label, however, unfortunately makes no mention of the Smith Family recipe since the company bought the recipe and all of the rights to it. The recipe will thus never be publicly known.[110] John Stasyshyn thinks the secret may include the use of long lasting Baldwin apples. Dick Smith however discounts that possibility saying, "hell we used to mix all kinds of apples together to make cider ..including rotten ones!" In the end the recipe is a mystery, just as is the mystery of how da Vinci produced his masterpiece, the Mona Lisa.

It should be noted that Lairds did not only buy the Smith recipe. Having obtained its license "Authorizing the Manufacture, Bottling, and Sale of 'Applejack', 'Apple Brandy', or other Alcoholic Beverages Distilled from Apples or other Fruit Juices" on December 6th 1933, the day after the repeal of Prohibition, it also bought out other prominent distillers in the county, most notably the huge Read family distillery in Blairstown which had begun operations around 1870 and had copper still with a 700 gallon capacity which could make seven runs (distillations) of whiskey in 24 hours.[111] Local names associated with applejack thus disappeared.

The Smith family can however be proud of its association with the

---

108 Source regarding Robert Vannatta: his son Harold. Source regarding the mailman: Charles Gorgas.
109 Source: Alan Apgar among others.
110 With one exception: John Stasyshyn told me he had obtained the recipe for what Walt Smith called his "Lady's Drink" which is as follows: To one gallon of 90-100 proof applejack add one pound of rock candy, a jar of maraschino cherries & juice, orange slices and ½ of a lemon. Let it sit for about a month, shaking it once/week. When the maraschino cherries turn white, it's ready!
111 See: *The History of Applejack or Apple Brandy in New Jersey from Colonial Times to The Present.* Henry Weiss, 1975 Trenton, NJ Dept of Agriculture p249-250 "The Read Applejack Distillery at Blairstown".

illustrious Lairds, who have been distilling whiskey in New Jersey since their immigrant ancestor arrived in 1698. George Washington was, in fact, aware of the Lairds before the Revolution, having written to Robert Laird requesting his recipe for "cider spirits" (ie applejack). Robert then served in the Continental army under Washington and his family supplied applejack to the Continental troops in response to Washington's view as to its benefits in boosting moral. Lairds later received License No. 1 from the US Department of Treasury in 1780 making it the oldest licensed distillery in the US. [112] In 1972 Lairds ceased its distillery operations in New Jersey, relocating them to Virginia. It does however continue to blend, age, and bottle its products in Scobeyville.

Top: The former post-Prohibition Smith brothers Distillery on Ridge Rd. Bottom: Local outlet advertisement for the Smith brother's whiskey (Photo courtesy of John Stasyshyn).

---

112 See Harrison, Karen Tina *Jersey Lightning*, New Jersey Monthly July 13th 2009 and Laird & Company Website at: http://www.lairdandcompany.com/ancestry.htm.

Of the next generation of Smiths, only one showed interest in the liquor business: Walt's son Lester, born in 1920. Dick remembered that Les once ran the Hutchison Pavilion which later became the S/S Diane riverside bar/restaurant and also once ran a village bar near the Hills Diner In Washington. After serving in US Navy during World War II, Les ran the Star Grill on Main Street in Washington, which he purchased in December 1945 with Charles Starker. In 1960 Les left decided to move to Alaska where he worked for many years with the Road Department.[113] Prior to this move he was a ski instructor in the Poconos and later captain of a ski team in Lake Placid New York.

One of Lester's close friends was Jesse Dalrymple, a Harmony Township Committeeman, who most likely learned to make applejack from the Smiths. Jesse would put out a barrel of hard cider in the winter and once frozen he would press an iron bar to its core to extract the alcohol. When he ran out of stock, he, like others, would pay Walt Smith a visit. He also made excellent cherry wine. Jesse's son Nelson "Nels" also knew Les very well and continued in his father's footsteps until he passed away in 2009 at age 93. Nels's stainless steel still was in fact made by his friends in a Belvidere factory's machine shop.[114] I myself have had the pleasure to taste my cousin Nels's delicious cherries steeped in moonshine. His younger brother Jesse Jr. ran a store in nearby Belvidere and would always keep a bottle of hard liquor or moonshine on the floor in the back which made him a lot of friends.[115]

In post-Prohibition Phillipsburg life returned to normal and the good times again began to roll in the resurrected salons which amounted to 28 by 1935. By 1940 there were 40 plenary retail consumption licenses, 3 for retail distribution, and 7 club licenses or one license for every for every 400 population![116] Still, there were scars, particularly with regard to the number of hotels which never recovered, amounting to only eight that year compared with the 25 which operated in 1918.[117]

---

113 Lester Smith's son Army Staff Sargeant Terry E. Smith was a war hero having died in combat in Vietnam on March 24th 1968.
114 Source: John Stasyshyn.
115 As told by Jesse Jr's daughter Dawn.
116 Two of the plenary retail distribution licenses were later cancelled that year. See *The Phillipsburger* article "Petition Supreme Court For Review On Liquor Stores" of 28 Mar 1940.
117 See *West's Easton PA and Phillipsburg NJ Directory of 1918* and *Polk's Easton PA and Phillipsburg NJ Directory of 1935*.

Joe McDermott remained busy, continuing his interstate smuggling even after prohibition when such interstate trafficking remained illegal. Dick Smith remembers accompanying John Piggott to the Neuweilers Brewery outlet south of Easton in John's 1929 Model A, which had no back seats and which they filled to capacity with cases of high powered beer. John was sent by Joe for supplies for his two bars, the Clubhouse Café and the Oakhurst and asked Dick to drive home which made Dick uncomfortable since interstate transport of alcohol at that time was illegal, but they made it over the bridge and back to New Jersey.[118]

Although Joe later sold the Clubhouse Café, he still owned the Oakhurst when Hurricane Diane hit the area in 1955. The bar was destroyed as flood waters rose to the roof and Joe's safe ended up in the middle of the river which resulted in a lot of talk about lost treasure and the lore about the safe still lying at the bottom of the river continues to this day. The truth however is that, fortunately for Joe, the safe was finally recovered. Joe had two daughters, Ann and Mary. In 1950, before the great flood hit, Joe was found guilty of income tax evasion. The indictment charged him with reporting a net income of $7,582.79 instead of $40,593 in 1943 and $8,951.76 instead of $49,845 thus an unreported net income of some $73,000, a big sum in those days![119] Consequently he spent over a year in jail. His daughters were told that he had gone on a long trip...

One thing about Joe had stuck in the back of my mind ever since Dick first told me about it in one of his early stories. It was his claim that Joe operated a pipeline which carried booze from Easton to Phillipsburg during Prohibition. I had known that during Prohibition the Seitz brewery not only produced a non-alcoholic cereal beverage it called "Seitz" but was repeatedly raided and charged with producing high-powered beer and was even padlocked for some time, but I had not come across any text references regarding a pipeline under the Delaware River. I was in the final stages of piecing together my story when by chance I met Richard Hope at the Easton Public Library. Richard had already published several books on Prohibition focused on

---

118 Such illegal interstate bridge traffic was reported in the local press see *Easton Express* article "Phillipsburg Center of Liquor Checking Through Last Week" of 29 May 1943. p8. That article however reported traffic in the opposite direction!
119 Figures as reported in The Phillipsburger article "Joseph McDermott Under Indictment by Federal Jury" of 19 January 1950 p1. Reference to his daughters are from a family member.

Easton, PA which required years of research. During our conversation I asked if he had ever heard of a Prohibition era pipeline which carried booze under the Delaware River from Easton, PA to Phillipsburg, NJ, and to my amazement he was fully aware of it. In fact, in one of his books he wrote that during Prohibition "most notoriously, the Seitz Brewery operation on Front Street actually produced illegal beer, in addition to legal soft drinks." and that "It avoided detection in part by piping the alcoholic product across the Delaware River to the American Horseshoe Company Works just North of Union Square, Phillipsburg. Air pressure from an electric compressor was used to force the beer under the River through a rubber hose line fitted together with iron couplings, similar to couplings found on railroad brake-hose lines." There was a racking room in the Phillipsburg Horseshoe Works where the beer was put into kegs, just as Dick had earlier told me! It had to be quickly shipped during the early morning hours to avoid detection by Prohibition agents or police.[120] This operation would have most likely begun in early 1929 since the American Horseshoe Works discontinued the manufacture of horseshoes after February 1st of that year. In addition, the Seitz Brewery had been padlocked for nine months from August 1926 until 18 May 1927 for producing high powered beer. By 1929 on to the end of Prohibition the brewery was connected with a string of breweries operated by the Reading PA "Beer Baron" Max Hassell. Considering Joe McDermott's "Club House Café" was only about one hundred yards from the Horseshoe Works, it is entirely feasible that old Joe was involved in the beer racking operation as Dick had said. Whatever Joe McDermott's involvement with the high-power beer racking operation at the American Horseshoe Works was, which may never be known, he was playing a dangerous game. This became eminently clear when Hassel, who was connected with the underground, was killed on April 12th 1933 by mob hit-men reputably linked with the notorious mobster, Dutch Shultz, who was later shot down himself by rival gangsters.[121] Seitz Brewery later lost its license on December 27th 1934 for using counterfeit crowns on its bottles instead of authorized crowns showing the State tax had been

---

120 Ref: *Easton PA: Special Projects* by Richard F. Hope Revised First Edition text c 2011, 2113 p199 & 200. Dr. Hope also refers to an interview of 2005 with Ed Koble then owner of the Wardell Restaurant in Phillipsburg, NJ who "told of sailing his boat in the 1950s to a point near Getter's Island, and confirming that the pipe across the Delaware was still in place."
121 For a fascinating biography of Max Hassel, see *Bootlegger Max Hassel, the Millionaire Newsboy* by Ed Taggert, Writer's Showcase, 2003.

paid. By September 1938, it was ordered to be sold under the Federal Bankruptcy act, and by November 1941 its building at Front and Bushkill streets in Easton was being dismantled to be replaced by an A&P supermarket.[122]

The American Horseshoe Works of Phillipsburg, NJ as viewed from Easton PA in the 1920s.

Brainards remained a lively place through the 1970s. The town's two bars, Dornichs' Tavern and Ropie's Brainards Café remained popular watering holes for area folks. Hunters and fisherman loved to go there to swap stories and old friends would meet to play shuffleboard and reminisce about the good old times. Back in April 1928 during Prohibition John Dornich was charged with unlawful possession of liquor and possession of gambling devices for which he had to pay $150 on the first charge and $50 on the second. His brother Steve also made the news in September 1932 when he had to pay a fine for unlawful possession of alcohol.[123] Ropie (his real name was John Sirotinak) became somewhat of a local legend for his strength. Many of his former patrons remember with awe his huge powerful hands and that he could take a nickel between the fingers of one hand and bend it!![124]

And as for the "King of the Bootleggers", after his nine-month

---

122 Ref: *Easton Express* article "Seitz Brewery Being Dismantled for A&P Store" of 26 November 1941 p1.
123 Ibid. Article "Defendants Enter Pleas" of 19 April 1928 for John and "Several Suspended Sentences Pronounced By Judge Runyon" of 17 September 1932 for Steve.
124 Amazing but true. As recounted separately by Ralph Raub and also by Lois (Tilman) Walsh who said her brother kept one of the nickels Ropie bent as a souvenir.

stint in the clinker and his last still blew up, Bob Clower eventually moved with his gal "Leaping Lena" off the mountain to New Village where they moved into a log cabin next to a gas station owned by Charlie Gilberti at the junction of Rt 57 and Edison Road. Lena died sometime after their move there. Although Bob most likely continued producing his famous brew, the outlaw became more subdued, spending the rest of his working career performing more mundane tasks as a member of the Franklin Township Road Department crew.

Montana Mountain applejack made from Baldwin apples remained in high demand, and was even prized at the state capital in Trenton. One story told to me occurred in the late 'and involved a high level government official who wanted to add a special touch to a State House reception by arranging to procure a case of Walt Smith's renowned applejack. Two of his bootlegger friends, one of whom was a penitentiary guard, were asked to deliver the cargo to Trenton. All went smoothly until, apparently sampling the quality of the product on the trip down; the two were stopped by State Troopers. They were about to be arrested and jailed until they explained they were delivering the cargo to the State House for a reception. Suspicious, the troopers called the State Police Barracks, which then called the State House which confirmed that the two were awaited. The two then had the pleasure of having a police escort to the Statehouse! [125]

---

125 Source: The son of one of the two individuals involved in the delivery. The identity of the actors in this story will not be identified at the request of this family member.

Chapter Thirteen
TIMES MAY CHANGE, BUT OLD TIMES LIVE ON

Much has changed since the wild and exciting days of Prohibition. Flannery's Tavern where Dick and Walt Smith went in search of Walt's fox hound is now closed. The Lanark Inn (ex Roxburg Hotel), the site where Walt Smith called out to his friends that someone had stolen his steering wheel, has gone through a number of recent reincarnations from "The Stagecoach", to "Kinneman's Pub", to "Bruhaha", to "Skoogies Sports Bar", to its current incarnation: "The Rock Creek Tavern". Across the street the Revolutionary period grist mill where Leo Lommason's still blew up one cold January morning in 1933 still stands as a historical landmark, although Leo is long gone having moved to Hackettstown in 1941 where he opened "Leo's Luncheonette". Leo sadly passed away in 1969 at the age of 79.[126]

Walt's favorite watering hole, "The Oakhurst Cafe" also still stands on the riverside in Hutchison but for the last 25 plus years carries the name of "The Hutch". Its current 97-year-old owner, Angelo Godino bought the property in 1980 and has been tending bar there ever since, known affectionately to his clients and friends simply as "Biz". Biz is one of Dick Smith's good friends. Dick is quick to point out however that Biz is just a kid since he is three months younger than himself. Biz's fascinating multi-faceted daughter Lisa often gives her father a hand at the bar. Although she has also worked as a tractor trailer truck driver, she is an accomplished artist/performer who sings beautiful Civil War ballads with a country band that has produced its own CD. Interestingly, Lester Smith was well known to Biz. There was a period when Les would come home annually from Alaska to visit and, while home, he would never fail to visit "The Oakhurst" his father's favorite

---
126 Ref: Obituary of E. Leo Lommason, *The Phillipsburg Star*, 3 July 1969.

watering hole, where he and Biz became fast friends. Biz remembers that during his annual visits Les would come with $1,000 to spend, all in 50-dollar bills. He couldn't be out of Alaska for more than 29 days though or he would lose the oil rebate that the State gave to residents there. Despite the changes in management, the Oakhurst remains essentially the same as it was when Joe McDermott ran it in the days just after Prohibition. Having a drink there along the Delaware River is thus a trip down memory lane.

Top: The Oakhurst Café today (now known as "The Hutch") looks much the same as when it was owned and operated by Joe McDermott.
Bottom: The S/S Diane before its demolition (courtesy of John Fulmer).

Like flecks of gold, bits of information would come to me to add to the stories I had already heard, answering lingering questions. Such was the case of the high powered beer pipeline that ran from the Seitz Brewery under Delaware River, which Dick Smith first told me that Joe managed but still left a question unanswered, who built it? One day, sharing the story with Bill Shepherd, to my surprise, he told me, "I know who it was!" He then told me that while employed at the Taylor and Wharton foundry in the 1960s, he worked with an older Hungarian man named Joseph Katrick, who would brag about his key role in its construction, saying that after being discharged from the Navy as a skilled welder during WWI he was sought for his skill and soon found himself gainfully employed welding the joints of pipe segments together. The work had to be done in the middle of the night to avoid detection. The pipeline remained undetected throughout Prohibition. Mr. Katrick has since passed and is buried in the Straw Church Catholic Cemetery in nearby Stewartsville, NJ.[127] Who hired him to do this work remains a mystery.

Just up the road from the former "Oakhurst Café" is an empty lot, once the site of "The Hutchison Pavilion" the bar once run by Walt Smith's son Lester. It was later owned and operated by Eddie Kehoe and his wife Ruth. This bar, like the Oakhurst suffered repeated damages from recurring floods. In fact, after the devastating flood of August 1955 caused by Hurricane Diane, Kehoe reconstructed it to look like a ship going upstream and dubbed it the "S/S Diane". It was a very popular place, with great pizzas! The property was later purchased by John Fulmer who ran it for about 18 years before selling it to the State of New Jersey under its "Green Acres" program. The riverside bar was demolished around 2010 and thus now only lives on in the fond memories of those who remember the good times they had there on the on the shore of the Delaware River.

Down in the little town of Brainards, life is humdrum compared with its glory days when it had a train station and the company store of the Alpha Portland Cement Company. During Prohibition it had been a wild place with a hotel and three saloons. Payday at the now closed Alpha Portland Cement Company across the river resulted Friday and Saturday evenings in heavy drinking and gambling followed by fist

---

[127] I also later discovered that the Kuebler Brewery on Route 611 just outside of Easton also operated a similar pipeline underground from its plant to a garage 150 yards away which went undetected until July 1927 when it was raided by Federal Agents and 125 half barrels of high powered beer were seized (see *Easton Express* article "Secret Pipeline from Brewery to Garage Unearthed by Agents" of 27 July 1927).

fights, stabbings, gun fights, police raids, and at least one murder,[128] but all is quiet now. The hotel is long gone. Most notable is the vacant lot where Ropie's "Brainards Café" once stood but has recently been demolished.

Top: The Roxburg Hotel/Lanark Inn as Walt Smith knew it.
Bottom: The Roxburg Hotel as Skoogie's Sports Bar

It is easy to pause while walking there and imagine the excitement of Walt Smith lying on his back on the (then) dirt road shooting pennies out of the sky. Down the road, Dornich's Tavern still stands next to the railroad tracks quiet and still, now a private residence. John Dornich passed away though in 1993 followed by his wife Ethel in 2014. Maryann Ignatz told me that her maternal grandfather, John Sipos, also lived in Brainards where he made high quality brandy which, at

---

128 An article of *The Easton Express* of August 11th 1924 entitled "Shooting at Brainards" reported more than 500 shots fired in two nights and buildings occupied by laborers riddled with bullets. Richard Galloway was murdered by John Thompson in February 1926. One notorious saloon owner, John Horvath, fled the county when faced with arrest and imprisonment (see *The Easton Express* article of December 20th 1924 "Horvath Has Left County").

the start of Prohibition, he would sell across the river in Martin's Creek PA to Dr. Reese, who was one of the "good doctors" who prescribed it to his patients.

Steve's Café in Phillipsburg is still going strong today, hosting monthly meetings of railroad enthusiasts, firefighters and alumni of local high schools, while also attracting others interested in local history. It appears that the historic tavern is now on track to be classified as a historic landmark. After Prohibition, the tavern still suffered from an occasional raid, but now by local thieves and not the Feds.[129] At the end of my extensive research and interviews regarding local bootlegging operations during Prohibition, the supplier of Steve Ignatz's speakeasy during Prohibition remained a mystery. The likelihood is high however that the mystery would have involved Steve's fellow Hungarians. Maryann agrees, particularly since she remembers John Fohr once telling her that he remembered her grandparents coming to visit his grandparents in their vehicle with the false bottom…

Up on Montana Mountain, the quiet seclusion and natural woodland and grassland is still sought after by those who seek privacy. It didn't surprise me therefore when Les Kober informed me that Ari Onassis, seeking privacy, was at one time looking at property in the area after his marriage to Jacqueline Kennedy. The log cabin behind the Kober farm once occupied by the nationally acclaimed accordionist Charlie Magnante Jr. is still standing and lived in. The mountain now also hosts a Buddhist Monastery, nestled in a wooded area off Montana Road, which few know about. It is a peaceful place where deer feel comfortable and seek refuge during hunting season.

Unfortunately, a number of bootlegger abodes have disappeared. Bob Clower's first house is now demolished and the spot is surrounded by heavy undergrowth and trees, many of which were laid prone recently from the force of Hurricane Sandy's winds. A lane to it is also blocked by overgrowth and bushes. There is now little left of his second house which lay off Youman Road other than a stone foundation with a large tree growing from its center. I had the opportunity to visit it and looked down into its stone foundation with awe imagining what all went on there. It is in a beautiful serene wooded location now covered with horse pastures, with a panoramic view from the nearby ridge overlooking New Village. It was clearly an ideal hiding place

---

[129] Two such thefts were reported in the local press, one in April 1940 when 2 bottles of liquor were taken and another in Sep 1941 when 10 quarts were taken.

back in the day! Nearby passes the same pipeline that Dick described to me where Jay Unangst had brought some good cheer to repairmen. I have been told that this pipeline which once conveyed oil now conveys communications via the fiber optic cables it now contains. The Denker family's home in nearby Low's Hollow is no longer there, nor is that of the Cathers', the Zollinski's or the Beers'. Most were destroyed with the construction of the Merrill Creek reservoir. While Dick brought alive the stories of these families, and the excitement of the times, others add to his memories. I was therefore fascinated to hear that when the supply of hard apple cider was depleted during the parties at Roy Beers' house, replenishment was easily had via what was known as "The Cider Trail", which ran from the mountain farms, discreetly down the mountain, direct to the Amzi/Earl Smith cider mill. There were also festive fall harvest get-togethers organized on the mountain organized by Rube Metz of nearby Stewartsville which may have required support via this Cider Trail.[130]

Although some houses are gone, the Magnante/Kober house still stands as do the houses of Walt, Harry and Amzi Smith and Amzi's cider press is still run by his descendants, the Apgars. Joe Steele's house also still stands as does that of his daughter Mildred and son-in-law Jay Unangst. All that is left of Hank Steele's shack however is a pile of rubble/broken pieces of wood and glass. Life goes on and time trudges forward.

Memories of the Smith brothers live on, including stories of how their moonshine was used for medicinal purposes. One of Charlie and Charlotte (Williamson) Richline's son's, Carl "Corky" Richline, remembers clearly that back when, as a little boy, he came down with a cold, his father went to Walt's brother Harry and returned with a pint of applejack, which he was told to drink with lemon and tea. Corky remembers drinking it all up and away went the cold.

Walt's legendary shooting skills also left an indelible mark on the minds of younger generations. John Stasyshyn, grandson of Charlie Richline, remembers with awe being at his grandfather's house as an eight year old boy in when Walt pulled up in his 1948/49 DeSoto and walked up to tell his grandfather that he was selling his applejack recipe, telling him "I can't roll barrels anymore". He then saw young John peeking at them behind a shed and went over to him asking "Are you Betty's boy?" Getting an affirmative, he then asked him "Did you

---

130 Source: Bill Shepherd.

ever watch Hopalong Cassidy when they throw a dollar up in the air and shoot it?" After John nodded that he had, Walt then walked to his car and came back with a shiny 38 caliber Smith and Wesson pistol and, taking a dime out of his leather pouch, he said before throwing it high in the air to shoot at: "If you can find it, when it comes down, it's yours!" Telling the story today, John says he waited with excitement for the coin to fall (which to him represented 20 pieces of Bazooka bubble gum) but admits with a laugh, "I never did find that dime!!"

John also knew about Walt's penny shooting in Brainards but had also heard that once when Walt was delivering whiskey there, one guy told him, "I could outshoot you any day!" Walt asked the barman for two 22 rifles and during the contest Walt hit every coin thrown in the air while his challenger missed every one. John also remembered that, instead of coins, Walt and Harry would at times shoot at blue tip matches at a distance to ignite them, or at the heads of nails tacked into a barn-side to drive them all the way in. He also told me of an old tree stump that once stood long ago on Ridge Road in Harmony that was well known to some local residents. Those in the know needed only to deposit $10 in the stump and, like magic, a gallon bottle of Walt's moonshine would be found there the next morning.

Then there was the story of a blowout/leak in one of Walt's two 500 gallon stills. Walt was not a plumber but needed to find one pronto. He therefore hijacked Jack Bishop of Asbury in the middle of the night to do the job. Bishop was blindfolded so he wouldn't know were he was going and soon found himself in the middle of the woods staring at two big stills. The damaged still was soon mended with silver solder and a patch and Bishop returned home a happy man since Walt, always a generous patron, sent him home with $100 and a gallon of whisky.[131] These stills were large. A modern-day bootlegger told me that it would take 125 hours (about five days) to run off 500 gallons into whiskey.

Down in Hutchison, Walt's cousin Joe Smith who remembered as a boy seeing lines of whisky jugs in Walt's barn ready for shipment asked Walt as a young man to sell him some but was always told there was none available. There came a day however when Walt needed a blood transfusion after an accident and Joe having the same blood type, readily volunteered to be a blood donor. Walt's gratitude for this

---

131 Source: John Stasyshyun.

act of kindness was unbounded and thereafter Joe received regular gifts of moonshine free of charge.[132]

In the course of my interviews, I was surprised to be told of a man on the mountain whose ancestors were participants in the Whiskey Rebellion of 1791! This led me to the home of Clair Krepps to be told the fascinating story of his German immigrant ancestor Christian Krepps who, after fighting and being wounded in the battle of Brandywine, moved to the Monongahela River near Brownsville, PA. Christian's son John became one of the leaders of the Whiskey Rebellion to protest against the excise tax on distilled spirits.[133] Claire told me, however, his family had very divergent views on alcohol and later split into what he referred to as the "Whiskey Krepps" and the "Prohibition Krepps" and that his father, a tee-toddler, was of the second branch. Claire however, like his good friend Dick Smith, enjoys the good things in life. While I was fascinated by Claire's knowledge of his family's history and his ancestor's involvement in the Whiskey rebellion, I was later amazed to discover that among the patriots buried in the Harmony Presbyterian Church cemetery lies a veteran by the name of William Gardner who, records show, was a Private during the "Pennsylvania Insurrection of 1794". This Pennsylvania insurrection was, in fact, the Whiskey Rebellion. Harmony Township thus had a combatant who fought on each side of this rebellion!![134]

In perusing newspapers, I also got a chuckle when I came across an article from 1925 concerning a Dennis Ryan who was placed in a cell Washington borough jail after being found intoxicated. By coincidence, a cask of contraband liquor had been place in an adjoining cell for safekeeping. The enterprising young man found a means of opening its spigot and the next day was found to be more intoxicated than when he was locked up![135]

One question which often came to my mind was what happened to the stills of the charismatic people I had been hearing so much

---

132 Source: Joe's daughter Joanne Smith who remembers her father often telling the story.
133 Another participant in the Whiskey Rebellion was Albert Gallatin, later Secretary of Treasury under Jefferson, who in 1802, oversaw the repeal of the hated excise tax on ardent spirits.
134 Ref: *Officers and Men of New Jersey in the Wars 1791-1815 NJ Adjutant General's Office*. Published by the Authority of the Legislature 1898-1903 p13. See also raub-and-more/harmony soldiers.html.
135 Ref: *The Phillipsburger* newspaper article "Prisoner's Fountain of Bliss" of 12 February 1925.

about. Where did they go? Were they sold for scrap metal[136] or are they hidden and/or still being used by descendants? Again Dick came to my rescue. When I asked him this question one day he told me "After Harry Smith died in 1959 from the self inflicted gunshot wound, his family held a big party and beat his still up into twisted metal and then sold it for junk.

OK, that's what happened to Harry's still but what about that of his notorious brother Walt? Walt, of course didn't just have one still; like Bob Clower, he had a number of them and spread them out. Two of 500 gallons which were each situated up a lane about 100 yards up the road from his post-Prohibition distillery have disappeared, with only two piles of charcoal and two chestnut trees to mark the spot. These may have been the ones that Jack Bishop was taken to repair.[137] Keg remnants and impressions marking where kegs were partially buried in the ground can also be found today in the fence-rows and woods behind Walt's house; hiding places that were carefully crafted to elude the revenuers. Then there was the still in Walt's basement; where did it go? Finally, I got the answer from one of Walt's descendants. After Walt passed away on April 19th 1972, Rosa had no use for it and sold it to Alan Apgar, the owner/manager of Apgar's Orchards and Cider Press and grandson of Amzi Smith. That still at least had found a good home that would ensure it's preservation for posterity.[138] When I mentioned this to Dick he already knew and told me that Alan had a back room which no one was allowed to enter. I had met Alan a number of times early in my research into the bootlegging history of the mountain folk of Montana Mountain but never thought of asking him about it. I was thus greatly saddened to learn that he had passed away on April 5th 2013 while I was travelling. I thus lost my chance to sit down with him for a lengthier conversation to fully tap his wealth of memories about his fascinating ancestors. It seems to me now though that Alan had been faithfully following in their footsteps, continuing their time honored traditions and that Walt Smith and his grandfather Amzi were smiling down on him.

---

136 Huge quantities of metal were collected in the 1940s in response to the war effort to produce armaments including cannons and cannon balls on the Belvidere Green which dated from the Revolutionary War. Copper was also highly sought after for munitions.
137 Source: John Stasyshyun who has visited the site.
138 As with Moses Allen, one of Walt's ledger books has been discovered is now in possession of a local family where it is prized and is being preserved as a fascinating memento of the past.

Once when reminiscing with Alan's wife Joan, her daughter Cindy and nephew Tim, Cindy mentioned something that surprised me: that Walt Smith was blind in one eye! Knowing Walt was an expert marksman/sharpshooter, I was amazed and doubtful on hearing this as I had never heard it from anyone before. I therefore turned to Walt's close friend Dick Smith for clarification. Dick at first told me he didn't remember Walt being blind in one eye, but after reflection he remembered the fox hunting story he told me earlier when after Dick shot at a fox, Walt called out in jest "You shot me! You SOB, you shot me!! I had only one good eye before and now have none!!" and remembering this he said, yes, it was true although he had never really taken notice of it since between friends such things mattered little. Bruce Unangst later again confirmed that Walt's had what is called a "dead eye" which he could not see out of and gave me a newspaper clipping which showed it was his right eye, meaning Walt shot with his left. When I showed the clipping to Dick, expressing my amazement at Walt's shooting skills with only one eye to shoot with, Dick replied matter-of-factly, "Well you only need one eye to shoot"!!

Stories of Walt's famed moonshine and bootleg activities keep turning up, thrilling listeners with his escapades. Before finishing this chronicle Bob Hamlen of Morris Park Phillipsburg, whose father Frank began the family heating oil business, told me that Paul Cahill, who ran Cahill's gas station where the Lopatcong plaza now stands was one of Walt's close friends. One day when, as a young man, Bob was out with the tanker delivery truck, his father contacted him by radio to go by Cahill's station to pick up some cases for his Uncle Eldin Norton which he said to put in the compartment on the driver's side in front of the tank. He instructed Bob to make sure that when he pulled up next to the garage the driver's side was not facing the road. The pickup turned out to be six to eight cases of Walt's applejack with four one-gallon jugs packed per case. Walt had a lot of friends and his cherished memory lives on.

Walt and his brothers' activities, while significant, certainly didn't gain the same level of attention and publicity as did the notorious Bob Clower, a newcomer from Pennsylvania and the Hungarians and it seems that none of the Smith stills were raided or destroyed. Perhaps, Levi Mackey, Warren County Sheriff from 1926-1929 at the height of the Prohibition would sound the alarm when the Feds were planning a raid as I had heard. I later found out that Sheriff Mackey would have had a good reason to keep the Smiths informed: his son Robert was married to Virginia Helen Smith, the daughter of Walt Smith's brother Clarence. He thus had outlaws for in-laws which put him in a delicate situation.

Levi's benevolence seemed, however, to touch not only the Smiths, but others as well, such as Gabe Kober and Emerick Wester, since my thorough review of press articles from the period revealed no instances whatsoever in which he personally participated in the arrest of any moonshiners or bootleggers on Montana Mountain. His obituary of 26 January 1961 did however, quote him as recalling "numerous raids he made in the company with the state police on speakeasies and "moonshine" plants in one of which, near Blairstown, he narrowly escaped being shot". His predecessor, William Jones who served from November 1923 to 1926 directly participated in the New Village raid that resulted in the arrest of 15 men and women in February 1924. Bob Clower's nemesis, the ubiquitous Federal Enforcement Officer Fred Kroesen, had actually moved his residence to Phillipsburg to give his full attention to his raids on which he was assisted by the town constable, Chris Rehfuss (who later faced criminal charges himself over an alleged theft of 14 barrels of beer in 1927). From 1930 Sheriff Mansfield Bowers and his deputy Emanuel Tiger directly participated in raids including those of the Westers in February 1930, of the Roxburg Hotel the next month, and of John Williamson in April of that year. The raid on Leo Lommason's still in 1933 was organized by the Feds. Levi by comparison seemed lenient and may indeed have helped to keep his neighbors out of trouble. Several individuals, including a family member in fact identified the officer posing in front of several large stills on the cover of this book as none other than Levy Mackey. Comparing this image with one acccompanying a 1926 campaign advertisement in the local press when he was running for sheriff, the resemblance is indeed striking as is the 1948 image of him which appears in his obituary of 1961.[139] Levi seems indeed to have been a good neighbor.

---

[139] One of these campaign ads with Levi's photo appears in the *The Star* newspaper (Washington, NJ) of June 3rd 1926 Section Two. Ref also Levi's obituary in *The Star*. January 26th 1961 p13.

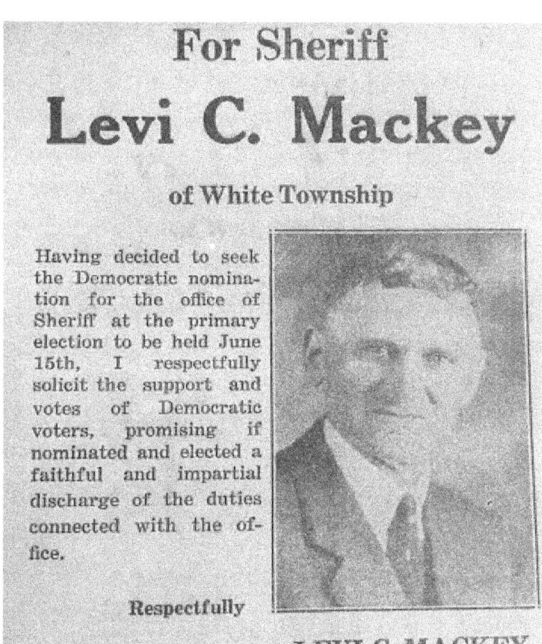

Levi Mackey Warren Co Sheriff 1923-29
Source: The Star Washington NJ Jun 3rd 1926

One last question about Walt lingered in my mind as I completed my work. Where did he learn to make his famous moonshine? Who was his mentor? A possible answer emerged from an Easton Express article of March 7th 1931 which referred to sentences imposed at the Belvidere courthouse. Among the offenders was a man named David Smith charged with violation of the prohibition law.[140] The name of Walt and Harry's grandfather was also David Smith. He passed away in December of that year, the much beloved patriarch of a large family. A tempting but unlikely possibility as there was another David Smith living in Phillipsburg at the time. It is much more likely that Walt acquired his expertise from his wife Rosa's uncle, who was none other than Amzi Smith, the very active but discrete bootlegger whose cider press sat at one end of "the Cider Trail", the back-road from the valley to the mountain. As for Amzi, he likely learned the art from his father-in-law Wendel Steele who, way back in 1894 was convicted of running a "disorderly place" where "choice wines of all kinds" were sold for 20 cents a quart.

Recalling that back on our first meeting Dick told me that everyone

---

[140] Ref: *Easton Express* article "Defendants Sentenced" of March 7th 1931 p8.

on the mountain was a bootlegger, my story cannot claim to be a comprehensive one. Thus, when Dick once mentioned that Jake Bungert, a dairy farmer who lived on Demeter Road, would take his milk by wagon to New Village in ten-gallon milk cans for onward transport to Kromer's creamery in Easton, PA he was most likely transporting more than just milk down the mountain, I now found it entirely believable since milk would have provided an ideal cover for a more valuable commodity. [141] As New Village was also the liquor transfer/delivery point for mountain bootleggers such as John Fohr, Jake could have very likely been a participant in this business, an assumption which seemed to be reinforced when Jake's grandson and namesake told me that while cleaning his grandfather's home after his passing, he came across an unusual object: a still which had miraculously survived through the years. Few of these precious objects have survived, in part because scrap, particularly copper, was collected to support the war effort during WWII. During Prohibition however, such instruments were very carefully hidden. I was not surprised therefore to later hear that the nearby town of Oxford, being a stronghold of the Klu Klux Klan during Prohibition, the Klan may have been involved in providing protection to some moonshiners.

In compiling this story, I backed up the reminiscences of my friend Dick Smith and others about the tumultuous prohibition period and the colorful local characters who rebelled against it by reviewing every issue of the "Easton Express" during the 13 years it spanned. In doing so I came across a raid the Federal Agents launched in New Village during which a woman named Mary Petrolati was arrested for unlawful possession and sale of intoxicating liquor. Remembering that Dick's first wife Pauline was also a Petrolati, I asked him if the two were in any way related. Dick smiled and then told me that Mary Petrolati was Pauline's mother. Dick thus, like Levi Mackey, had an outlaw for an in-law! [142] He then told me that the barber shop in New Village where he would hang out as a kid was that of Pauline's brother, John.

This account of the escapades of Dick Smith's friends from days gone by cannot close without recording here one of his toasts which

---

141 Dick remembered that as a young man he had a horse also named "Dick" on which he would race Jake Bungert driving his milk wagon down the mountain.
142 Pauline had, in fact, accompanied her mother to her arraignment for the illegal sale and possession of alcohol for which bail was set at $400. After Pauline assured the judge the bail would be provided that same morning, her mother was released. Ref: *Easton Express* article "Find Enough Rum In New Village Section to Float a Battleship" of 15 Feb 1924 p8.

he rattled off with the speed of a 20-year-old trapped in a 97 year old body.

"Here's to it, to do it,
When you get to it, to do it,
And if you don't get to it, to do it,
May you never get to it, to do it, again. *Na Zdorovie*"!

My reply was always the same: "*Mir I Druzhba*",
another Russian toast meaning:
Peace and Friendship!

Dick Smith making a toast

Postscript

Dr. Benjamin Rush (1746-1813) was an enlightened Jeffersonian whose multifaceted contributions to the birth of the American nation place him firmly in the Pantheon of our founding fathers. Apart from being a preeminent America medical professor and practitioner, as a member of the Sons of Liberty in the 1770s he assisted Thomas Paine in editing his revolutionary pamphlet published anonymously in January 1776 and suggested to Paine that it be called "Common Sense". He later signed the Declaration of Independence as a member of the Continental Congress from Pennsylvania and the following year became the Surgeon General of the Continental army during the Revolutionary War. In 1784, three years after the war, he published his most famous pamphlet, "An Enquiry into the Effects of Spirituous Liquors upon the Human Body, and their Influence upon the Happiness of Society" written after returning from a trip to Carlisle to observe the progress of Dickinson College whose charter (the first such charter after Independence) he signed the previous year. The indelible mark the trip made on him is reflected in his diary where he wrote "the quantity of rye destroyed and of whiskey drunk in these places is immense and its effects upon their industry, health and morals is terrible" [143] and, writing to a friend he admitted being stunned by the proliferation of "stillhouses" built by frontiersmen on their land and commented on how it would be to the credit religion and the honor of society " in abolishing whiskey distilleries and converting them into milkhouses".[144]

Putting his views into practice, it was in fact Rush who, as part of a physicians temperance movement, lobbied Congress to pass the notorious whiskey tax which was intended to finance the new government

---

143 *Hawk, D.F. Benjamin Rush: Revolutionary Gadfly* Indianapolis Indiana. Bobbs Merrill Co; 1971. p303.
144 B. Rush to Wm. Linn, May 4 1784; see Butterfield LH, ed *Letters of Benjamin Rush* Princeton NJ: Princeton University Press, 1951 p270-273.

while promoting public health but which resulted in the Whiskey Rebellion which caused Washington so much grief. Later, his essays, compiled in a volume in 1798 reflected the American Enlightenment by urging penal reform, condemning capital punishment, proposing an American tailored education system, demanding the abolition of slavery and also calling for a temperance movement.

Benjamin Rush however was a realist and as such never advocated prohibition. His focus was rather on educating people about the hazards of Ardent Spirits (distilled alcoholic beverages such as whiskey, gin, and rum- previously used strictly as medicines) as opposed to beer or wine. In his 1874 pamphlet, he considered beer, in fact, a "wholesome beverage" which "abounds in nourishment". As a member of the American Enlightenment, who lived by the scriptures, Rush considered human reason as the ultimate source of perfection in this world and that education was a key element to this end.

On one occasion and only one did Benjamin Rush ever consider the option of an official prohibition of the use of ardent spirits. It came to him as a dream which he later described to his dear friend John Adams in a letter of September 16th 1808. In the dream he told Adams he had been elected to the office of president of the United States which he accepted only because it would give him the opportunity to act decisively on his "long cherished hostility to ardent spirits". After persuading Congress to pass a law "to prohibit not only the importation and distilling but the consumption of ardent spirits", he is faced with enormous opposition and petitions to repeal the law but he refuses to act. A "venerable but plain looking man then appears in his office and explains to him that no matter how reasonable the law might seem, it is not working. The man then suggests that Rush retire from the presidency and go back to his professor's chair to amuse his students with his "idle and impractical speculations" or to his patients "and dose them with calomel and jalap". Rush then awoke abruptly " by the vexation... in being thus insulted" and was relieved to find it had been only a bad dream.[145]

If only the only the US lawmakers of the 1920s who decided to legislate morality had had the same dream that Benjamin Rush had in

---

145 Rush B. to J. Adams, September 16th 1808. In: Butterfield LH, ed. *Letters of Benjamin Rush*. Princeton, NJ: Princeton University Press; 1951: p976-980.

1808! [146] Moreover, had these legislators learned from American History they would have seen that Prohibition had a precedent when alcoholic spirits were prohibited in the Georgia Colony in 1733. For nine years lawlessness ran rampant with the neighboring Carolinas running huge quantities of liquor into Georgia to fill the gap until the folly was acknowledged and the law was rescinded n 1742.

Having not learned from history, the folly in enacting "The Great Experiment" was thus repeated at national level with dire consequences and the moral debate continues to this day. In the words of Benjamin Rush, "The American War is over, but this is far from being the case with the American Revolution"!

In closing, it is perhaps appropriate to repeat the immortal words of another great American, Mark Twain, who prophetically said about the folly of the zealots responsible for the 18th Amendment to the US Constitution: "Nothing so needs reforming as other people's habits. Fanatics will never learn that, though it be written in letters of gold across the sky, it is the prohibition that makes anything precious".

---

146 It is worth noting that the Soviet government also worked with an Anti-Alcoholic Society to reduce liquor supply and consumption during the same period as the US Prohibition. It was said at the time that "Sovietism and alcoholism do not go together" and that the country should eventually become liquorless. Unlike the US; however, Russia enacted no prohibition laws the approximate $750 million spent on alcohol annually. (see *Easton Express* article "Cutting Down Liquor Supply" of December 30th 1930 p20).

In Memoriam

It is with deep regret and sorrow that I must say in closing that Dick Smith, my dear friend, passed away on June eleventh 2016. The shining light of his memory began to fade in his final days but his humor did not. He had often asked me if he would see the published book before he passed, but this was not to be. Publishing a book is not an easy task. This book however now finally stands as a monument to a wonderful, kind-hearted man who loved his friends and family and was loved and respected by all who had the pleasure of knowing him. He has now gone through the window to the past and an eternity of togetherness with his companions of bygone days.

Annex i: Excerpts from Easton Express/Easton Argus press articles concerning Robert "Bob" Clower 1923-1932

Monday December 3, 1923:
STILL RAIDED AT MONTANA Alleged Owner to Be Arraigned Before U.S. Commissioner

Fred J. Kroesen..a Federal prohibition enforcement officer, arrived… on Saturday and proceeded to Montana… where he raided a still on the premises of Robert E. Clower. The alleged owner of the still will be arraigned before William P. Tallman…Mr. Kroesen was accompanied on the raid by a Phillipsburg constable... there were two stills on the premises, one …of thirty gallons, the other almost twice as large. ..the enforcement officer destroyed about four barrels of what was regarded as good stuff, along with several barrels of rye mash.

Tuesday December 4, 1923:
FEDERAL AGENT ACTED FIRST Took Man Into Custody At Unexpected Time

Fred J. Kroesen, a Federal enforcement officer, acted first…. just when the state authorities were prepared to act…. concerning the arrest of Robert Crowder (sic), charged with … possession of two illicit stills at his home at Montana, Warren county.

There is a wide difference of opinion regarding …. the right of the Federal officer to act in the manner he did is likely to be thoroughly aired at a hearing …this week before Judge Harry Runyon at Belvidere….

Following the arrest of Crowder he was arraigned before Supreme Court Commissioner J.I. B.Reiley…. and .. entered bail for his appearance before Judge Runyon at Belvidere.

In connection with the raid at the Crowder home, …not less than three barrels of liquor were destroyed …with about five barrels of rye mash.

Prosecutor Smith stated today … his office had been at work on this very case and had called the state police… a warrant having been issued, but that Kroesen acted without a warrant, and without notifying the office of Prosecutor Smith.

... Prosecutor Smith stated that this is not the first time that Federal officers have entered Warren County in such a manner to act against alleged violators of the liquor laws, and from the tone of his remarks there is a difference of opinion regarding the manner in which state and Federal officers work.

Friday December 7, 1923:
CLOWER PAYS FINE FOR VIOLATING PROHIBITION LAW

Three bottles of perfectly good red "licker" were destroyed in open court at Belvidere this morning when Robert Clower, of Low's Hollow, appeared before Judge Harry Runyon and entered a plea of guilty of illegal possession and sale of liquor. A fine of $150 was imposed and Clower was warned by the court to refrain from further participation from such business. The three bottles of illegal stuff that were brought into court were poured in a wash bowl.

Monday March 10, 1924:
MOONSHINER FIRES SHOT AT FEDERAL ENFORCEMENT OFFICER Bob Clower, Low's Hollow Desperado, Dodges Five Shots..As He Ran From His Still

Bootleggers ... sometimes take desperate chances. Robert E. Clower took a chance this morning at his home near Low's Hollow, NJ when he drew a revolver and fired two shots at Fred J. Kroesen, a Federal prohibition enforcement officer. That Clower is not charged with murder is due to his poor marksmanship. One bullet ... passed through a sleeve of Kroesen's overcoat.

Kroesen and Clower clashed .. while the enforcement officer was struggling to gain possession of the revolver, Clower is alleged to have fired another shot... Constable Chris Rehfuss of Phillipsburg was making a search of the house, and hearing the shots and the noise... hastened to the assistance of Kroesen. Entering the room he found the men in a clinch and he was quick to see that Clower had a revolver. Federal officers do not carry gun....

"Throw down that gun or I'll kill you." said Rehfuss, and Clower, when he saw the danger that faced him, complied but not until he had squirmed about the room holding ... Kroesen all the time, until he reached a door.

He then dropped his gun like a licked criminal, and ran, but not in a straight path, and the five shots that Rehfuss sent after him failed to take effect.

Clower has been in trouble before and …is said to be in line … for a hearing in Federal court on… violations of the prohibition laws. Recently he was fined in the Warren county court.

Clower came to this section about two years ago…little of his past record is known, still the officers who had dealings with him declare that he is a desperate character. His arrest is expected in a short time.

Clower's wife was not at home when the officers arrived… Satisfied that the bootlegger and .. gunman would not return for a time … the officers made a search of the house. They confiscated a still capacity 50 gallons and …brought back to Phillipsburg … five gallons of moonshine booze and a lot of mash. This afternoon Officer Kroesen appeared before Justice of the Peace Ray M. Weiss, of Phillipsburg, and swort to a warrant charging Clower with assault with intent to kill.

Tuesday January 27, 1925: **CLOWER TO GO TO TRIAL**
Must Answer Charge of Shooting at Officer Kroesen

Robert Clower, who was arrested at Low's Hollow several months ago, during a raid at his alleged moonshining establishment and … alleged to have shot at Fred J. Kroesen, a federal prohibition enforcement officer is to be placed on trial in the United States District Court at Trenton … tomorrow morning.

…Constable Chris Rehfuss .. is summoned to appear as witness. Rehfuss accompanied Kroesen and the officers on the raid of the Clower place and according to the story told…Clower was found in the house and interfered with the officers in performance of their duty. He is alleged to have had on him a big revolver and threatened the officers… firing a bullet from his weapon. The bullet passed through the clothing of officer Kroesen.

Rehfuss jumped to the assistance of the prohibition enforcement agent and Clower was quickly subdued. He was then placed under arrest.

Friday January 30, 1925: **CLOWER CASE DISMISSED**
Jury Acted on Advice of Judge Rellstab, Trenton

By direction of Judge Rellstab, of the Federal court... at Trenton ... the jury ... called to hear the case against Robert Clower... on a charge of illegal manufacture of intoxicating liquors, and... with assaulting Fred J. Kroesen, a federal prohibition enforcement officer, returned a verdict of not guilty.

The trial consumed but little of the time ...after Judge Rellstab was informed by counsel for Clower that the raid ... had been made by the officers without a search warrant, he directed that the charges be dismissed. The verdict of not guilty was returned by the jurors without leaving their seats.

Constable Chris Rehfuss, who was with Kroesen when Clower's place was raided, was present. In the fight that took place, Clower is alleged to have fired a shot from a revolver at Kroesen, the bullet passing through the officer's clothing.

Monday August 23, 1926: **BOB CLOWER TAKEN AGAIN**
Arrested for Driving While Drunk; Will be Held for Smith

Robert Clower, better known to hundreds of people as "Bob" Clower was arrested last night on a charge of driving an automobile while intoxicated and was taken to Washington by Deputy Sheriff Clarence Garis of Phillipsburg and William K. Teel a state motor vehicle inspector. He was taken into custody on the outskirts of Phillipsburg.

Clower has been in serious trouble on a number of occasions. A few years ago he resided in Easton ...employed as a foreman by contractors on building construction and later... entered the bootlegging game.

Early in 1923... he located near Low's Hollow. The officers heard reports regarding the manner ...his place was being conducted so a raid was decided upon. This was to have been handled by the state police... But about the time the police arrived, Fred Kroesen... also got there. Clower managed to make his escape but he was apprehended later on and arraigned in court at Belvidere and a stiff fine was imposed. Clower evidently decided that he would continue his elicit business...other reports came to the authorities and after he had been arrested and arraigned in the United States District Court, he was discharged, Judge Rellstab holding that the officers had no right to conduct a raid without a search warrant.

Again Clower returned to Warren county and again reports were received concerning him, and, according to the authorities, he was reputed as putting out pretty good whisky. A raid was staged and Kroesen was placed in charge.

Kroesen then maintained a residence in Phillipsburg. He went to the place with other officers. He was recognized by Clower and in a fight that took place Clower is alleged to have shot at Kroesen. The latter declared that a bullet fired by a revolver in the hand of Clower pierced his trousers.

The fight resulted in Clower making his get-away, but he was soon captured and ... brought before the United States District court only to be acquitted second time. For a couple of years Clower appears to have been operating quietly. If he continued ... manufacture of his whisky, he managed to keep this knowledge from the authorities but recently after he moved to a section of Montana mountains, there came word of his operations.

While Clower was driving an automobile along the Belvidere road last evening, his machine ran against a car standing in the front of the home of George Clymer. The car is owned by a son of Superintendent Hemmingway, of the Standard Silk Company's Mill, Phillipsburg. The Hemmingway car was forced onto the sidewalk and was considerably damaged. Deputy Sheriff Garis placed Clower under arrest, turning him over to Inspector Teel... Teel had been summoned from his home in Washington when it became known that the man taken in charge by Garis was 'Bob' Clower. Teel took Clower to Washington and .. plans to arraign him before a justice of the peace .. this evening.

When S.C.Smith Jr. of Phillipsburg, Assistant Attorney General, was advised of the arrest, he communicated with the sheriff's office and Inspector Teel stating that he would prefer charges against Clower for illegal possession and transportation of liquor. It appears that a gallon of moonshine was found in Clower's automobile.

October 6, 1926: **CLOWER WOULD BE LAWYER
But Judge Runyon Appointed Mr. Dahlke to Defend Him**

Robert E. Clower, when arraigned ... in court at Belvidere yesterday, entered a plea of not guilty to a charge of unlawful possession and transportation of liquor. Clower has been residing in the Montana mountains.

After his plea had been recorded he was asked if he had engaged a lawyer, and to the surprise of the judge, lawyers and many others present the defendant announced that he would handle his own case. Judge Runyon has heard defendants make this remark before and …certain defendants who thought they knew all about criminal law made pitiable spectacles of themselves and at times they wasted much valuable time. For this reason Judge Runyon appointed John Dahlke to represent Clower when the trial will be begun, October 13.

Thursday October 14, 1926: **CLOWER CONVICTED**
Once More Montana Man Is Convicted on Rum Charge

Robert E. Clower, who resided in the Montana mountains… and who was indicted on two counts, transporting liquor and unlawful possession, went on trial at Belvidere this morning and a few minutes later the jury returned the verdict of guilty on the unlawful possession indictment. Judge Runyun had ruled the other indictment out. Clower was arrested August 22 last. When the verdict was returned, he was remanded to jail for sentence.

The first witness called was County Clerk Reese, who produced records of the court to show that Clower was arraigned December 7, 1923, and entered a plea of guilty to a charge of unlawful possession of intoxicating liquor. He paid a fine of $150.

George Clymer, residing along the Belvidere road, and Joseph Hemingway, of Phillipsburg, testified .. they were in Clymer's home the evening of August 22, when they heard a crash. They investigated and found .. Clower's automobile had crashed into the car of Hemingway. Both declared that Clower appeared under the influence of liquor… Clymer told that he found Clower attempting to remove a jug of whisky from his machine. The alleged whisky was taken from Clower and retained for a time by Clymer.

W.K.Teel, motor vehicle inspector, and Deputy Sheriff, Clarence Garis placed Clower under arrest. Teel and Garis testified that they recovered a jug of whisky from Clymer who said that it had been taken from Clower. Teel, asked if he had tasted the whisky, he replied that he had and that it was "bum stuff".

Clower gave his age as 51 years. He testified that two of his sons had visited him the day of the accident and that he had driven them ... so that they could board a trolley for their home in Easton. Returning ..home, he testified, he encountered two automobiles on the pike. One had lights but the other did not, and he swore that the accident was unavoidable. He denied that he had been drinking and .. swore .. he had not carried liquor in his automobile. If liquor was found in his car it was placed there by someone else, he declared. Clower swore that the first he saw the jug of whisky was when it was brought from Clymer's home.

Thursday May 8, 1930: **CLOWER TO FIGHT CASE
Pleads Not Guilty and Is Held for Trial; Other Actions**

Robert E. Clower, a resident of Harmony township who has been before the Warren county and other courts on numerous occasions this morning pleaded not guilty to an indictment charging him with unlawful possession of intoxicating liquor as a third offender. He said that he has no lawyer and does not intend to hire one. He told the court that he "intends to take care of his own case". He was remanded to jail to await trial.

Wednesday May 21, 1930: **BOB CLOWER APPEARS IN COURT WITHOUT ATTORNEY**

With Judge Harry Runyon presiding, criminal court opened at Belvidere at 10:30 o'clock this morning and the first case called was that in which Robert Clower of Low's Hollow is charged with unlawful possession of intoxicating liquor.

When Clower was arraigned to enter a plea several days ago an indictment having been returned against him by the grand jury, he pleaded not guilty and then announced that he had decided to be his own attorney.

At the opening of court this morning, he announced that he was prepared to conduct his own defense and without ado the case was started. S.C, Smith, Jr. representing the State.

When adjournment was taken at noon, a couple of State witnesses had been heard, but up to this time Clower was very little in evidence.

The defendant is being tried as a third offender of the prohibition law. In 1923, he was convicted and paid a fine. In 1926, he was again convicted and served a short jail sentence.

Thursday May 22, 1930: 'BOB' CLOWER FOUND GUILTY
Conducted Own Defense on Dry Law Violation

"Bob" Clower, arrested several weeks ago when a raid was conducted on his place at Low's Hollow and who was later indicted by the Warren county grand jury on charges of unlawful manufacture and possession of intoxicating liquor, went on trial at Belvidere yesterday before Judge Harry Runyon and was convicted by a jury during the afternoon.

Clower conducted his own defense but there was little of a spectacular nature during the trial. S.C. Smith Jr. represented the State. Clower will be arraigned for sentence at a later date. He has already served a term in jail for dry law violation and on another occasion, following conviction he paid a fine.

Friday June 6, 1930: NINE MONTHS FOR CLOWER
Must Also Pay Fine of $500 as Third Offender

Found guilty by a jury recently in criminal court at Belvidere as a third offender of the prohibition laws, Robert Clower who had been holding forth a long time in the vicinity of Low's Hollow, was brought before Judge Runyon at Belvidere this morning and was sentenced to serve nine months in jail and pay a fine of $500.

Clower has already paid a fine for liquor violations and he has also served a term in prison. When in court for trial and couple of weeks ago, he was his own counsel, but he made little impression on the jury, a verdict of guilty of unlawful possession being returned against him.

July 12, 1932: GIANT HELD FOR STABBING OXFORD YOUTH AT CLOWER MOUNTAIN HOME **New Village Man Charged With Assault As Result Of Free-for-All Row In The Hills**

Clarence Miller, 21 years old of Oxford was stabbed three times in a fight, at the "Bob" Clower place in the Montana mountains, Franklin Township early this morning. He is in Warren Hospital, Phillipsburg

... condition is reported as fair. Miller sustained wounds of the neck, chest and upper left arm. The blade of the knife that was used in the assault broke from the handle, being removed from Miller's body at the hospital.

As a result of the stabbing William Lambert, 41 years old, of New Village tipping the scales at not less than 230lbs, is charged with the assault and was committed to the county jail without bail to await the result of Miller's injuries.

Lawrence M. Kappler of Oxford who drove the automobile in which Miller was brought to the hospital was later charged with operating a motor vehicle while intoxicated and in default of a fine of $200 and costs, he was committed to jail for 90 days. His license to drive will be suspended for two years.

Although the trouble occurred at Clower's place, he has not been arrested, the authorities feeling that he was not responsible for the trouble since the stabbing took place close to the .. house and before an Oxford party had an opportunity to enter the dwelling. Clower has been in trouble a number of times in the past several years, once for an alleged assault on Frederick Kroesen, a revenue officer.

When word was received by the police from Warren hospital that Miller had been delivered there, County Detective Warder and officers Silverthorn, Stabp, Martin, Tarpel, and Moyer were assigned to the case and later on they went to the mountain home of Clower. They rounded up Mr. and Mrs. Edwin Brown of Oxford; Kappler, and then found Lambert at his New Village home.

The authorities say that the Browns, Miller, and Kappler had been at a party early last night, and then decided to visit the Clower place. When the hearing was conducted before Justice Weiss, this morning, Kappler was first called. He entered a plea of not guilty to a charge of operating a motor car while drunk, but the police produced a statement from a physician to the effect that when examined by him, Kappler was under the influence of liquor.

Lambert was next called, being charged with the assault on Miller. He admitted ...drinking, and then told that there was a free-for-all during which he was knocked down and that he only defended himself. He remembered reaching into one of his pockets and then identified the knife as his property.

Mr. and Mrs. Brown testified that when they reached the Clower place, in company of Kappler and Miller, they saw Lambert standing close to the house and there was another man present... Brown said that there were two other automobiles in the yard and that as his party drove in Lambert made unfavorable remarks regarding Mrs. Brown. Brown told Lambert to be careful, and then, with the unidentified man, moved on toward the Clower house.

In a short time Miller approached him stating that he had been hit. Brown saw blood on his shirt, and then decided that he should be taken to the hospital. He did not see Lambert stab Miller, but, he swore, Miller stated that he had been hit by Lambert. Mrs. Brown told of seeing the several men grouped together, but did not witness the assault on Miller.

When the trip to Warren Hospital was under way, with Kappler at the wheel, the automobile ran on a bank and was partly wrecked but was able to continue on to Phillipsburg.

August 4, 1932: **POLICE RAID CLOWER PLACE**
"Big Bob" Was Found Sleeping, With Gun in His Room

County Detective Wieder and troopers from the Washington station of the State police early this morning visited the home of "Big Bob" Clower in the Montana mountains of Warren county and placed Clower under arrest.

A couple of weeks ago there was a rumpus at the Clower place, during which a man was stabbed, and from that time on, it appears, the authorities were planning a visit to Clower. Clower expected such a visit, he told the authorities, after he had been taken into custody.

For a long time past the police say they have been receiving complaints regarding activities in the vicinity of the place kept by Clower, and as a result of the stabbing there the opinion was general that there was strong drink on the premises.

The officers approached the place without attracting the attention of Clower, and had no difficulty in entering his bedroom through an open window. When Clower awoke and saw the officers, his first remark was that he expected such a visit. The police found a gun in the room.

A search of the building revealed according to the officers a big still in the cellar, and they confiscated quantities of whisky and wine. Clower was taken to the lockup in Washington to be held for a hearing this afternoon.

The police reported that there appeared to be no one but Clower in or about the building.

August 18, 1932: **Population of County Prison Reduced By Session of Court Large Number of Defendants Paid Fines and Secured Their Liberty: Some Sent To Institutions**

Judge Harry Runyon spent nearly an entire day in special sessions court at Belvidere yesterday when a large number of defendant men and women entered pleas of guilty ... Robert Clower, arrested in the Montana mountains was listed as a third offender by Prosecutor S.C. Smith who represented the State to all cases and he was sent to jail for nine months, a fine of $500 also being imposed.

Annex ii Phillipsburg Speakeasies Active During Prohibition

Phillipsburg Speakeasies active at the start of (& during) Prohibition with owner(s)/ notable events

Bar name	Street Address	Owner/Proprietor	Event /date
American House	24 N. Main St.	John Kravecz	closed 5 Oct 1920
			raided 18 Jul 1925
	-	Steve Kravecz	raided 10 Jul 1932
N Main St Café	12 N. Main St.	Geo Stasak	fined $1,000+ 9 mo jail
			27 May 1925 for
			liquor violations
Ivy Leaf Café	12 N. Main St.	Howard Swain,	closed 5 Oct 1920
		Jacob Jaceviez	raided 1 Aug 1925 & arrested;
			booze was in fact vinegar
		Steve Kops	raided 26 Jan 1926
Saloon/café-Rest	511 S. Main St. (Union Sq)	Harry Doyle	indicted for illegal sale liquor; found not guilty 21 Jan 1921
	.	Alfred Carty, Joseph Teleka	arrested/jailed 7 Jul 1925 arrested 30 Oct 1929; beer, whiskey seized
Delhigh Hotel	33 S. Main St. (Union Sq)	Palmer Heller Wm. H. Walters	closed 5 Oct 1920 flooded in Nov 1932
Hotel/saloon	45 S Main St.	Wm. B. Ulmer	closed 5 Oct 1920
Eagle Hotel	360 Chambers St.	Wilson Beitler	fined $50 for sale of whiskey 29 Sep 1920
		Bert Gilson	closed 5 Oct 1920
Cedar Park Hotel	377 S. Main St.	Julius Rosenfelt (later held Fed. Wholesale Liquor Lic.)	closed 5 Oct 1920
Roma Restaurant	384 S. Main St.	Joseph Losco	raided 22 Jul 1932 12 kegs liquor & 2 stills found)
Imperial Hotel	390 S. Main St.	N.F. Pines	closed 5 Oct 1920
Hotel/saloon	45 S. Main St.	William Ulmer	closed in Oct 1920
Saloon	475 S. Main St.	John McLaughlin & Harry Friedman	closed 5 Oct 1920 22 May 1925

			Mrs Friedland arrested & Furnished $500 bail
Andover Hotel	733 S. Main St.	Harry Friedland	raided 20 Jun 1924; Scotch whiskey confiscated Friedland arrested furnished $500 bail
2nd Ward Hotel	489 S. Main St.	B. Gilluly	
Washington House	504. S. Main St.	Mike Chipiuiskis	raided 27 Jul 1924
		M. Rasukas	raided 18 Jul 1925
		Steve Parrish	convicted 21 Nov 1927 of alcohol possession
4th Ward Hotel	566 S. Main St.	Louis Kish	tried for liquor sale May 1925; prison 1-5 yrs in Mar 1927
American House	500 S. Main St.	Steve Kravecz	saloon ordered locked 21 Jan 1925
		Nick Wynovich	jailed 8 Feb 1928
Morris House	766 S Main St.	Steve Ignatz	raided 12 Jun 1926
Phillipsburg Hotel	212/14 Main St	Harry Smith	closed 5 Oct 1920; raided 16 Aug 1924 (next to police HQ)
		Louis Segaro	raided 4 Feb & 18 Jul 1925 illegal sale/possession. Bail $1,000.
Green's Hotel	38 Market St	William Green	closed 5 Oct 1920
New Hub House	84 Sitgreaves St.	I.N. Miller/Edw Kobble	closed 5 Oct 1920 raided 4 Feb & 18 Jul 1925
		George Stasak	arrested 6 Feb 1925
Restaurant	34 Sitgreaves St.	Joseph Baumgartner	raided 26 Jul 1930; 11 men arrested
Stockton House	Mercer & Stockton Sts.	W. Guest Wm. Swick	closed 5 Oct 1920 raided 4 Feb 1925
Fifth Ward Hotel	273 Chambers St.	Milton Mount	closed 5 Oct 1920
Reliance Hotel	247 Chambers St.	Mrs. Chas Singley	closed 5 Oct 1920

Name	Address	Proprietor	Notes
Lee House	Union Square	M.O.J. Hile	closed prior to Sep 1920
Club House Café	Third & Broad	Joseph McDermott	raided 4 Feb 1924 beer seized. Bail of $1,000 provided.
Hotel Columbia		W.H. Carey	
Bachelor's Inn	331 Chambers St	Edwin H. Clause	raided 20 Jun 1924 whiskey/gin found. Clause arrested
		Joseph Stamus	raided 13 Dec 1930 arrested/fined $250 17 Jan 1931
Sargeant Hotel	Center+Roseberry Sts. (near Ingersoll Rand)	William Hale	raided 19 Dec 1927
		Joe Takach	raided 26 Jul 1928/charged with illegal possession/sale of Liquor
		Stanley Daniels	raided 30 Sep 1932; jailed for 60 days in default of $100 fine.
Saloon	266 Heckman St.	Edgar Fraufelter	closed 5 Oct 1920
		Louis Travaglini	raided 15 Dec 1930

Private homes:

Steve Recbo	2 Mill Street	arrested 11 Apr 1921 still, 5 gal whiskey, 2 barrels of mash seized.
Joseph Kilpatrick	S. Main St	arrested 6 Feb 1925
Paul Solaki		" "
Shandor Barber	104 Sitgreaves St.	raided 18 June 1926 5 bottles beer seized.
Septra Cuva	112 Sitgreaves St.	raided 12 May 1927. white Mule & Wine found
Alfred Tagleattchi	54 Fox St.	raided 14 Jul 1932 basement full of home brew
Louis Travaglini	Heckman St.	raided 13 Dec 1930 fined $150 on 17 Jan
Joseph Stamus	Chambers St.	raided 13 Dec 1930 fined $250 on 17 Jan
Mike DiMatteo	" "	raided 13 Dec 1930 fined $100 on 17 Jan
Frank Spurio	350 Chambers St.	raided 15 Aug 1932; 800 bottles beer seized
Rorla Coglerli	304 Warren St.	raided 29 Dec 1931

Mary Vosler	112 A Sitgreaves St.	raided 27 Aug 1931 charged with keeping "disorderly house"
Joe Losco	354 S. Main St.	raided 28 Jul 1932 Beer wine &whiskey were found throughout 3-story building. Two stills totaling 75 gal capacity seized. Value $4,000.

Brainards

Warren Hotel	John P. Horvath	raided 9 Dec 1924, arrested with 6 customers 5gal.+2 qrts moonshine, 2 barrels wine seized Plus gambling devices. Earlier had furnished $1,000 bail for atrocious assault.

Annex iii: Brief Chronology of Events published in the Easton Express/Easton Argus

(note: Dates are publication dates; Phillipsburg, NJ is indicated as "P'burg)

Date

1920 **(under term of County Sheriff Thomas Hayes of Belvidere)**

Jan 17 "Prohibition Now the Law of the Land of Liberty"; Took effect the previous midnight.
Now illegal to manufacture, sell, or give away liquors containing over one half of 1% percent alcohol.

May 25 NJ Gov. Edwards' manager denies liquor interests are "underwriting his campaign for President".

Jun 7 Fed. Prohibition Amendment and Enforcement Act passed by Congress is held constitutional by Supreme Court.

Sep 13 Belvidere Judge Stewart: Federal law cannot change the human heart or change human nature; nevertheless, the law of the land "must be administered with severity/firmness".

Sep 29 P'burg: Wilson Beitler, owner of Eagle Hotel fined $50 for selling four glasses of whiskey at 50 cts each to Moses Thorp on July 4th and ordered to close. Mayor warns other hotels/saloon owners.

Sep 30 Affect of Volstead Act: A number of former licensed saloons are now closed including the two largest hotels in town, the Phillipsburg Hotel & the Lee

House. Belvidere: More drunk men on the streets previous Saturday than since the wet days of the Farmers' Picnic.

Oct 5 P'burg: Fifteen more saloons closed: Palmer Heller's Delhigh Hotel, Howard Swain's Ivy Leaf Café', Harry Smith & Wm. Green's Market St. saloons, I.N. Miller's Hub House, N.F. Pines's Hotel Imperial, W. Guest's Stockton House, John McLaughlin's saloon on S. Main St., Steve, Kravecz's American House, Julius Rosenfelt's Cedar Park Hotel, Milton Mount's Fifth Ward Hotel, Mrs. Charles Singley's Reliance House, Wilson Beitler's Eagle Hotel, & Edgar L. Fraufeller's saloon on Heckman St.

Nov 8 P'burg: Law & Order League cites extensive bootlegging in local industries. Liquor is manufactured in private homes/sold on the premises & large-scale gambling is ongoing in town.

Nov 17 P'burg: Barrel of Whiskey stolen from Federal licensed warehouse of C.G. Smith

1921 (under term of County Sheriff Thomas Hayes of Belvidere)

Jan 21 New Jersey ratifies the 18th Amendment

Jan 22 P'burg: "Saloon Man Acquitted": Harry Doyle, indicted for selling liquor the previous May and Nov., is acquitted.

Jan 29 P'burg: Anti Saloon League inspects Imperial Hotel ("a regular dive".."filthy condition"..."very active business") & the DelHigh Hotel in Union Square. Liquor sold openly.

Feb 19 P'burg: Three liquor violators cited; Mayor Smith criticized for inaction by Law & Order League.

Mar 9 Beer declared a medicine like wine under medical prescription; Anti-Saloon League disapproves.

Mar 16 "Beer in Practically Unlimited Quantities for "Sick"; Prohibition Commissioner: Physicians given full authority/discretion to prescribe such quantities of beer as they deem necessary.

Mar 30 Prohibition Bill passed by NJ Senate over Governor Edwards veto.

Apr 22 P'burg: Four barrels of whiskey stolen in hold-up at warehouse of Oscar Smith at 55 N. Main St

May 2 NJ's Van Ness dry law took effect midnight Apr. 31st but no change was noticeable.

Oct 4   P'burg: 25 quarts of whiskey dumped into sewer /Delaware River at Union Square after arrest of Syrian, Sam Maree.

Oct 10   New Village: Three Hungarian moonshiners (James Gurzo, Nick Sharkey, & John Smith) arrested and wine, liquor & stills seized. Andrew Vargo & wife of Valley View P'burg fined $300 for still. Cement bags stolen from Edison Cement Co. found at their home.

Oct 25   Beer prescriptions permitted for sick (also wine and spiritual liquors).

Nov 2   NJ Democrats push for repeal of Van Ness Enforcement Act; Republicans support it. (It enabled trial without trial by jury & set restrictions on medical prescriptions of spirituous and vinous liquors).

Nov 13   "How Long will Phillipsburg be the Paradise of Bootleggers?"

Nov 23   Anti beer law signed by Pres Harding (outlawed medicinal beer); Nothing in the Volstead Act precluded prescription of beer as medicine.

Dec 3   P'burg: Alcohol seized on Marshall St. declared unfit for hospital use destroyed; An earlier seizure was dumped into Delaware River.

1922   (under term of County Sheriff Thomas Hayes of Belvidere)

Jan 10   Edwards calls Van Ness Enforcement Act an instrument of oppression; Urges repeal & use of
                    trial by jury.

Mar 10   NJ ratifies the 18th Amendment on 9 March

Nov 8   P'burg: Twenty-two barrels of liquor seized at N. Main St. storehouse of Oscar G. Smith, a member of the Seeley Drug Co. which manufactured a medicine known as "Know No Pain".

Dec 6   Edwards: "Prohibition, like charity should start at home"; Proposes drying NJ Senate & House of Reps. as 1st step in enforcing 18th Amendment.

Dec 14   Bootleggers combine efforts/reap profits in holiday trade/Smuggling rush across US borders with Canada & Mexico.

Dec 29   "Queen Susan" held/charged with delivery, sale and possession on intoxicating liquors confiscated at "Monkey Bar" in New Village NJ. (had speed truck)

1923 (under terms of County Sheriffs Thos. Hayes of Belvidere & Wm. Jones of Blairstown)

Oct 4 — Poison Booze cost the US 2,000 lives lost in the first nine months of the year.

Oct 18 — Coolidge stands steadfast in Dry Law enforcement

Dec 3 — Fed Prohibition Office Fred Kroesen raided still of Bob Clower. Discovered two stills 30 & 60 gals. Destroyed 4 barrels of "Good Stuff" & two barrels of rye mash.

Dec 4 — Bob Clower arrested for 2 illicit stills, 3 barrels liquor, and 5 barrels Rye mash all destroyed by Fed. Enforcement Officer Fred Kroesen without a warrant or informing Prosecutor Smith.

Dec 7 — Bob Clower pays $150 fine after pleading guilty to illegal possession and sale of liquor and "three bottles of perfectly good red licker" were destroyed in open court being poured into a wash bowl.

1924 (under term of County Sheriff Wm. Jones of Vail)

Jan 3 — New Village: Three bootleggers (Julia Vanya, Steve Rotz & Louis Radke fined $50 each for illegal possession of liquor.

Jan 7 — Susan, Queen of Easton Syrian colony arrested at the Monkey House in New Village; Paid fine of $400 for illegal possession/sale of liquor.

Jan 16 — "Scofflaw" wins nationwide prize as epithet to "stab awake drinkers' consciences".

Jan 26 — Bob Clower Place Raided Again. Kroesen confiscates a 100 gal & two 50 gal stills and 16 barrels of mash.

Feb 4 — Moonshiners Antonio Guidi and August Sartini arraigned on charges of illegal possession of liquor. Guidi paid $150 bail/ Sartini $300.

Feb 5 — Oxford NJ: Milton Beers goes on wild rampage fighting with "anyone and everyone"; imbibed liquors "stronger than his name implies". Earns 60 days in county jail.

Feb 14-5 New Village: In biggest liquor raid involving 15 men & women police confiscate one 5-gal keg, three 5-gal jugs, 9 barrels of wine/ whiskey, 90+ bottles of alcohol, brandied peaches/cherries and one slot machine. Arrest warrants issued for: Mr/Mrs Jos. Piani, Mr/Mrs Louis Sabatini, Mary Petrolati, August Sartini, Nazarene Santini, Frank Sinopli, Tony Guidio, Paoli Ricardi & others. Amount seized considered "Enough to float a battleship".

Feb 19   New Village: Bootleggers pay fines amounting to $1,435 (bail given on 28 Feb.)

Feb 20   Arthur Sheats fined $300 and jailed for illegal transport of whiskey; His rum running vehicle is confiscated/sold.

Feb 27   Pburg: New Village booze (12 Barrels,10 kegs, 50 bottles of whiskey/wine) poured into sewer by Deputy Police Chief Garis; "brandied" cherries re turned to A. Sartini.

Mar 10   P'burg bootlegger Charles Lowitz arrested; bail set at $5,000; Bob Clower, "Low's Hollow Desperado", fires at Fred Kroesen then dodges five shots from Fed. Enforcement Officer as he runs from his still.

Apr 12   P'burg: Fake Dry agents take possession of a carload (150 Half barrels) of high powered lager beer seized earlier in the day at the Lehigh Valley RR freight yard at P'burg labeled as "Fish Perishable".

Apr 22   Alcohol insanity increased 1,000% nationwide under Prohibition due to poison Liquor.

Apr 26   P'burg: Stanley Renshaw of P'burg found dead from "alleged" poison whiskey

May 9   P'burg: Fed agents Kroesen & Gautest of Newark HQ raid saloons of Wm. Green on Market St , Doyle & Gaughran in Union Sq. , & Wm Ulmer S. Main St.

Jun 21   P'burg: Andover Hotel & Bachelor's Inn raided; whiskey, gin, & a slot machine seized.

Jun 21   P'burg: Ceremonial funeral of John Barleycorn held in front of courthouse. Five barrels &15 gallons liquor poured into 7th St sewer flows on to the Delaware River

Jun 24   Brainards Saloons raided: Warren Hotel of John P. Horvath & saloon of Frank Nemeth. Large amount of liquor & bottle labels/caps and slot ma chine confiscated from Horvath. Bobbed hair girls assist in raids also in Alpha and P'burg.

Jul 19   P'burg: Kroesen raids four saloons: John Kravecz's on N. Main St., Harry Smith's on Market St., Louis Segaro's, Phillipsburg Hotel & Eddie Kobble's Hub house. The Pequest House in Belvidere also raided.

Jul 28   P'burg: Washington House raided on 27th; 10 men/1 woman arrested including proprietor Mike Chipluiskis & his wife; fines imposed.

Aug 3   P'burg: Proprietor of Ivy Leaf Hotel, Jacob Jaceviez, arrested. Liquor confiscated found to be vinegar.

Aug 11   Brainards: Over 500 shots fired in 2 days. Gambling aimed at relieving colored cement plant employees of their earnings accompanied by stabbings and shooting matches.

Aug 16   Five Raids in Warren Co. on 15th included Eagle Hotel & Phillipsburg Hotel in P'burg. Owners: Bert Gilson & Harry Smith.

Dec 3   P'burg: After bandits raid on gambling House (Ivy Leaf Hotel) officials/townspeople are stirred to action.

Dec 9   Brainards: During police raid. Five men & two women taken into custody: saloon owner John Horvath, Robert Robertson, and four "colored". Large quantities of whiskey, wine along with a slot machine, punch board and dice seized.

Dec 15   P'burg: Police raid restaurant of Edward Rupell in Union Square. Rupell arrested after seven gallons+ two quarts whiskey found.

Dec 20   Brainards: John Horvath saloon owner left the county prior to court appearance for illegal sale and possession of intoxicating liquors. Non-appearance at court bail of $1,800 bail to be attached. Also charged with assault & battery and maintaining gambling devices in his place of business.

Dec 30   P'burg: Bandits raid Ivy Leaf Hotel gambling joint on N. Main St./hold up gamblers & make off with over $8,000. Townspeople criticize police inaction regarding this known gambling establishment.

1925   **(under term of County Sheriff Thos. Jones of Blairstown)**

Jan 1   P'burg: Joe McDermont arrested at his place 3rd & Broad Sts.; Four glass Jugs seized and $1,000 bail paid.

Jan 20   Warren Co Grand Jury inquest returns 9 indictments re December raid on Ivy Leaf Hotel by bandits. Presentment concluded police failed to take action regarding Prohibition infractions. Proper rules and procedures were established but were not enforced and Chief of Police, as Director of Public Safety, was responsible.

Jan 21   P'burg: The American House saloon of Steve Kravecz ordered padlocked by Fed. judge.

Jan 27   Bob Clower goes to trial on the 28th to answer charge of shooting at officer

Kroesen.

Jan 30   Bob Clower case dismissed because raid on his home was performed with out search warrant.

Feb 2/3 P'burg: In biggest raid ever 5 saloon owners arrested: George Stasak, Howard Swain, Wm. Ulmer, Wm Green, Louis Kish along with 5 private house owners James Blank, Segondo Piani, Luigi Serafini, Luigi Peanelli, and Paul Castiglia. Two truckloads of booze of all kinds is seized. Castiglia & Kish provide bail.

Feb 5   P'burg: Six more saloons raided. Bail provided by 6 defendants Joe McDermott, Louis Segaro, Wm. Swick, Edw. Kobble, Jos. Kilpatrick, & Paul Solaky.

Feb 6   P'burg: Leak suspected regarding the raid on saloons since no whiskey found in any of the six places raided. P'burg police were suspected but vigorously deny guilt.

Feb 11   Brainards: Richard Galloway is shot dead by John Thompson, " colored" after a crap game gone bad.

May 8   Lows Hollow: Moonshiner Arrests: Thomas Bianco & Joseph Uberseder; Liquor seized; each paid $1,000 bail.

May 12   Seitz Brewing Co. at corner of front and Bushkill Sts. sold.

May 16   Three Brainards widow women Teresa Nemeth, Mary Pordon and Annie Dorerics fined $150 for illegal possession/sale of alcohol

May 22   P'burg: Rae Friedland & Andover Hotel bartender Wm. Herbert arrested/ provided $500 bail each.

May 25   P'burg: Louis Kish charged with sale of alcohol got one to five years in State prison + fine $1,000

May 27   Writ of Error filed for Louis Kish & George Stasek of P'burg; Both re leased on Bail; Henry Mountain of Oxford charged with illegal possession of alcohol.

May 28   Joe McDermott fined $550 + 30 days in jail suspended for good behaviour.

Jul 1   Bob Clower nemesis Fred J. Kroesen Prohibition Enforcement officer & Group Head at NJ HQ in Newark resigns.

Jul 7   P'burg: Warrant issued for arrest of Alfred Carty proprietor of saloon 511 S.

Main St.

Jul 18   P'burg: Washington House raided; whiskey and gin found; Proprietor Mike Rasukas absent.

Jul 28   P'burg: Joe Takach, Prop. of Saloon near Ingersoll-Rand, charged with il legal possession/sale of liquor & as "keeper of a disorderly house". Paid $500 bail; 12 men/2 women charged with frequenting this "disorderly house" were fined $3-$9.

Sep 12   P'burg: Grocery store of Joseph Huff (client of Steve Ignatz) on S. Main St. raided. Two containers of whiskey seized.

Sep 19   P'burg: Seventy of 175 barrels/half barrels seized by Fed. Agents were removed from a locked storehouse on 130 Delaware Ave. and warrants are issued for the arrest of 3 men.

Oct 16   P'burg: Arrest of John London, Gang leader behind Ivy Leaf Hotel holdup/robbery.

1926   (under terms of County Sheriffs Thos. Jones & Levi Mackey)

Jan 27   P'burg: Steve Kops proprietor of the Ivy Leaf Hotel charged with illegal possession of liquor furnishes $500 bail.

Jan 29/30 New Village, NJ: Sam Crotzo stabbed by Joe Pirko after drinking. Pirko jailed.

Feb 15   Belvidere: One of the biggest booze raids conducted on 13 Feb. Arrested: Fannie and Roy Smith, Andrew Muchlin, Kline Hess (candy store owner), Fletcher Blazier (barber). Bail set at $500 for each. Roy Smith had a still. Hess cited for permitting gambling on his premises. Police erred in raiding butcher Gordon Richards instead of tailor Joseph Richards..

Feb 25   P'burg: Two Penna. RR carloads labeled "cereal beverage" containing high powered beer confiscated by Fed agents.

Apr 30   Lafayette College students spend $50,000/year on liquor

Mar 1   Nicolas Wynovich (owner of the America House in P'burg) fined $200 for unlawful possession of liquor; on 2nd indictment (unlawful sale) sentence of 30 days in the County jail was suspended on condition that he close his business.

May 17   Spectacular raid on Seitz Brewery. Fifty employees backed against wall at gunpoint by
Feds. Twelve arrested including Brewery president. One hundred barrels of

high powered beer and 1000 gallons in vats confiscated.

Jun 12 P'burg Police Chief Gorgas visits places of Steve Ignatz (Morris House), J.P. Smith and Louis Kish; No liquor found.

Jun 19 Shandor Barber place on Sitgreaves St Pburg raided by police; 5 bottles of beer seized. Belvidere: Steve Kopa fined $500+ 3 mos. Jail for 2nd offense.

Jul 1 Seitz Brewery under 24 hour watch of Fed Agents to ensure compliance with Govt. regulations.

Aug 3 P'burg: Police raid home of Henry Roncoroni on Warren St. One bottle gin, 2 gallons wine & 4 gallons liquor confiscated.

Aug 13 Easton: Seitz Brewing Co. seized by Dry agents and again closed. Charged with bribing Dry agents.

Apr 26 P'burg: Surprise Police raid on Washington House and Andover Hotel. No liquor found.

Aug 23 Bob Clower Taken Again. Arrested for "Driving While Drunk"; hits car of Joseph Hemingway, Superintendent of the Standard Silk Co. Mill, Phillipsburg at home of Geo. Clymer. Clower charged with illegal possession & transport of liquor since a gallon of moonshine was found in his car.

Oct 6 Bob Clower pleads not guilty to charge of unlawful possession & transport of liquo. Informs Judge he would be his own lawyer, but Judge appoints Dahlke to defend him.

Oct 14 Jury finds Bob Clower guilty on unlawful possession charge. After crash into Hemingway's car, Clymer & Hemingway considered Clower under the influence of liquor and Clymer observed him removing a jug of whiskey from his trunk which Clymer took from him. Clower vehemently denied being intoxicated or having any whiskey jug in his trunk.

Nov 9 Easton: Seitz Brewery padlocked until May 1927

1927 (under term of County Sheriff Levi Mackey)

Mar 4 P'burg: Louis Kish sentenced to one to five years in state prison and to fined $1,000 for violation prohibition enforcement laws.

Mar 10 P'burg: Truck containing 12 half barrels of high powered beer seized by police. The driver,Theo Smith, had PA DMV license issued to the Lehigh Beverage Co. The truck was taken to Belvidere and turned over to Sheriff

Mackey.

May 12-3 P'burg: Police raid home of Pietro Cuva 112 Sitgraeves St. & confiscate 11 barrels wine, seven 5-gallon cans of "White mule" and 20 qrts. wine in bottles. Cuva arrested for unlawful possession of intoxicating liquors but later declares alleged liquor was in fact vinegar.

May 18 Easton: Padlock removed from Seitz Brewery after almost 1 year. Manufacture of cereal beverages of not to exceed one-half of one percent authorized.

Jul 7 New Village: Virginia Marcelli arrested. A large amount of alleged whiskey confiscated and a five and ten gallon still. Bail of $500 provided by August Bevilacqua. Fifty half barrels of high powered beer seized by Feds in P'burg. Truck and cargo taken at River & S. Main Sts.

Jul 11 Truckload of beer seized on Phillipsburg-Washington Rd. Two men from Brooklyn arrested and held in default of $300 bail each.

Jul 28 Easton: Feds discover secret pipeline from old Kuebler Brewery to a garage 150 yards away enabling transfer of large quantities of beer to where it was kegged/loaded on trucks.

Oct 29 New Village: Two 700-gallon stills confiscated. Three men arrested (..Stevens, Jack Schwartz, &Lester..)

Nov 21/24 P'burg: Joe McDemott & Constable Chris Rehfuss indicted for conspiracy regarding seizure of 20 half barrels of beer from John Hickey. Defendants plead not guilty. Trial began on 24th.

Nov 29 Trial of Joe McDermott & Constable Rehfuss on conspiracy to obstruct justice byspiriting away 20 half barrels of beer after its seizure is suddenly declared a mistrial due to suspicion of jury tampering.

Dec 19 P'burg: Police Chief Cutsler & officers arrested William Hale of Sergeant Hotel near Ingersoll-Rand. Found 3 bottles whiskey, 1 keg with 4 gal. wine, and 12 bottles of beer and gambling devices. This was the forth raid by police there.

Dec 21 P'burg: American House raided. Proprietor Nick Wynovich arrested. Fifteen gal. whiskey, wine & punch boards/ dice found. Wynovich charged with unlawful possession of liquor; furnished $500 bail.

1928   (under term of County Sheriff Levi Mackey)

Jan 17 P'burg: Police Chief Walter Kutzler arrests James W. Smith for driving while intoxicated.

Feb 9 P'burg: Nick Wynovich of American House jailed for unlawful possession/

sale of liquor. Proprietor Kravecz pays $500 bail, then withdraws it, and Wynovich is jailed.

Mar 8   P'burg: Truck stolen from Ed McNulty of Colby Place found overturned/wrecked nea Washington NJ with kegs/broken bottles strewn about emitting an odor of beer.

Apr 19 Harmony: John Piani of Roxburg Hotel, found guilty of possession intoxicating liquor fined $100. Steve Stacek with place on N. Main St.Pburg, guilty of same offense, fined $50; Brainards: John Dornich of Brainards found guilty of same offense and possession of gambling devices fined $150 for the 1st charge and $50 for the second.

May 23 Easton: The Delaware Beverage & Cold Storage Co. (old Kuebler Brewery) closed by Dry Administrator after repeated raids & violence against Fed agents. Beer in production/storage is destroyed & license to produce "cereal beverage" revoked. One RR carload shipped from Easton to Pittsburg la beled as "salted pork" contained beer.

Aug 28 P'burg: John Bartos grocery store on Sayre Ave. raided and a quantity of high powered beer and half pint of whiskey found. Bartos was arrested for illegal possession of liquor (under terms of County Sheriffs Lei Mackey & Mansfield Bowers)

Feb 14 Harmony: Jack Zocchi held under $350 bail/ Three barrels of homemade wine for domestic use is confiscated. Complaint made by Steve Starkey.

Mar 12 P'burg: Six arrested in Cherry alley garage raid. $10,000 in bottling equipment destroyed

May 7   New Village: "Negros in Drunken Brawl". Two men and one woman jailed after stabbing of John Lucey.

May 10 Harmony: Two large stills 500 gal each value $2,000 destroyed in mountainous section of Twp. Four barrels of liquor poured from containers.

Jun 20 N.J. Congressmen: There is no Bootlegging in NJ judging from paucity of complaints. Rep. Chas. Eaton's secretary: "Warren & Hunterdon Counties are the only real bone dry counties in the State".

Aug 29 Truck driven by Joseph Azzalina of Pburg loaded with 21 half barrels of beer seized near Oxford. Bail $500. Truck and cargo turned over to Sheriff Mackey of Warren Co.

Aug 31 P'burg: Purcel St Raid. Thirty half-barrels & 12 barrels seized by Fed Agents at Washington Extract Company. Contents of barrels destroyed/

poured into street. Three men fled into woods.

Nov 13 New Village: Frank Piani convicted of illegal sale and possession of liquor and a still. He, David Elms, and Frank Landon were arrested in Sept. after a raid on a still in mountains behind New Village..

Nov 14 Wm. Obrien of Oxford charged with driving a car with seven 10-gallon kegs of Applejack. Charged with illegal possession of liquor (3rd offense) and illegal transport (1st offense); Found guilty by jury.

Oct 30 P'burg: Joseph Teleka of 511 S. Main St held on $500 bail for possession of beer & liquor during raid on 29 Oct.

Nov 22 Sentences at Belvidere: Wm. Obrien fined $200 for illegal transportation of liquor. Auto Seized. Frank Piani of New Village fined $100 for illegal possession of liquor.

1930   (under term of County Sheriff Mansfield Bowers)

Feb 24 Harmony: Huge 1,500-gal still seized in the barn of Emerick Wester on Montana Mt.; Wester & his 3 sons arrested with one other. A 1,500 gal still was seized. Another still located and seized at the Bianco farm near Ingersoll Dam.

Mar 4   Harmony: Three men arrested during raid at the Roxburg Hotel: The proprietor, John Pavoni, for unlawful possession of liquor at $1,000 bail, Harry Bowers of Bangor for resisting an officer and Wm. Hawk of Brainards for disorderly conduct. Officers found 30 barrels of hard cider, beer, and a still in a barn.

Mar 15 Warren Co.: five places raided including in Belvidere: Joseph Richards, Market St. (1,000 bottles of beer & whiskey found), Walter Haycock, Prospect St. (whiskey found). Parties involved escaped on approach of police.

Apr 11 Harmony: John Williamson property raided by Sheriff Bowers. Still and liquor confiscated. Williamson jailed in default of $500 bail.

May 5   Dwight E. Avis becomes the 17th Prohibition Administrator in 17 years.

May 8   Belvidere Court: Bob Clower, Emerick & Victor Wester and George Washington enter pleas of not guilty on charges of illegal possession of liquor

May 16 N.J. Sen. Morrow wants repeal of 18th Amendment.

May 22 Harmony: Large 300 gal still and 60 gallons of liquor+ mash valued at $1,800 seized on Montana Mt above Roxburg.

May 21/22   Bob Clower, acts as own attorney at trial for being third offender of prohibition law, having been convicted/fined in 1923 and again convicted/jailed in 1926. The following day a jury again found him guilty of unlawful possession and manufacture of intoxicating liquor.

Jun 6   Bob Clower sentenced to 9 months in jail and $500 fine for the 3rd offense violation of prohibition law.

Jun 18   Dwight Morrow (R) defeats Sen. Frelinghuisen in Warren County NJ primary for US Senate. (He later wins this Senate race but dies in October the following year).

Jul 19   Two modern 1,000 gal rye whiskey stills seized in Warren Co. One operated by 2 men on Gabe Kober's farm on Montana Mt. Kober was arrested although he wasn't operating the still. Unable to furnish $1,000 bail each, the three were jailed.

Jul 24   Harmony: Big Still is found/destroyed on Montana Mt. Harry Emery and Daniel Kane later arrested when 3 gallons of whiskey, suspected from the still is found in their vehicle.

Jul 25   P'burg: Walter Macauley of P'burg charged arrested with truck containing 20 cases and 6 half barrels of beer on Belvidere Rd. Bail $1,000.

Jul 26   P'burg: Saloon of Joseph Baumgartner, Sitgreaves St., raided. Baumgartner & 10 others arrested. Baumgartner charged with "conducting a disorderly house" and fined $100. Others fined $2 each..

Dec 30   P'burg: Raids of Louis Fravagline, Joseph Stamus & Mike DiMatteo go to Grand Jury. Home of Rorla Coglerli of 304 Warren St. raided. A still and alcohol was seized; fined $100.

1931   (under term of County Sheriff Mansfield Bowers)

Jan 17   P'burg: After guilty pleas re Dec 13th raid Joseph Stamus of Bachelor's Inn fined $250, Louis Travaglini fined $150 & shoemaker Mike DeMattio $100 when liquor found in shop. Gabe Kober farm owner fined $100, Rude Madrigal still operator $150, and Daniel Devick, laborer $100 for liquor manufacture.

Feb 23   Edward Kalber NJ Police convicted of extorting Earl Smith of Harmony re still operation. Sentenced to 3 years.

Mar 5   Chris Piazza of P'burg arrested in Newark with 1,500-gal still & seven huge vats filled with mash.

Apr 25   P'burg: Antonio Pipperado raided/ arrested & charged with maintaining a disorderly house. Five gallons of alcohol + 15 bottles of wine found. Fined $25.

May 16 P'burg: Anthony Piperata & Horace Buchman found guilty of Possession of liquor; Piperata fined $500; Buchman's sentence suspended.

Jul 24 Harmony: Still destroyed/liquor seized on Montana Mt. Harry Emery & Daniel Kane later arrested when 3 gallons of whiskey found in their car and held on $500 bail. Whiskey presumed to have come from the seized still.

Aug 28 NJ leads both PA & DE in Third Prohibition Dist. in amount of alcohol seized in previous 13 mos.

1932 (under term of County Sheriffs Mansfield Bowers & Russel Doyle)

Mar 18 NJ Leads District in Liquor seizures with in Feb with sixteen large distilleries raided plus 239 seizures and 283 arrests. Fifty-five stills and 38 vehicles were seized in NJ compared with 137 stills and 75 vehicles overall for district..

May 25 Former NJ Governor Edward Stokes advocates repeal of 18th Amendment.

Jul 9 P'burg: Police raid 2 houses on Mercer St. of Geo Carpenter & Angelo DeThomas. Two gallons of liquor seized/each fined $100 plus costs for "keeping disorderly houses".

Jul 11 P'burg: police raid on 24 N. Main St saloon of Steve Kravecz; Eleven men & women arrested. Kravecz fined $100. Two private residences on Mercer St. also raided.

Jul 29 P'burg: police raid Roma Restaurant on 384 S. Main St. & arrest owner Joseph Losco; Seized: two copper stills, two 50 gallon barrels of whiskey & other barrels/jugs. Five more barrels of whiskey found underground in yard. Some poured into sewer. Losco committed to jail in default of $500 bail.

Aug 1 P'burg: Sargeant Hotel raided. Owner Stanley Daniels jailed in default of $100 fine. Six others fined.

Aug 5 P'burg: Attempt at force entry into Police HQ basement to steal seized whiskey & 100 gallons of seized whiskey poured into sewer by police.

Aug 6 P'burg: Police raid homes of Geo Carpenter & Angelo DeThomas of 202/04 Mercer St. In 2nd offence, six barrels whiskey + 24 gal jugs of alcohol unearthed. In default of $1,000 and respectively, both jailed.

Aug 15 P'burg police raid home of Frank Spurio 350 Chambers St. seize 800 bottles home brew.

Nov 15   J. Russel Doyle replaces Mansfield Bowers as Warren County Sheriff

1933   (under term of County Sheriff Russel Doyle)

Jan 5   Roxburg NJ: Raid on Leo Lommason. A 500gal still found. Five arrested

Apr 1   NJ legislators agree on temporary beer sale law. W.C.T.C. objects. Sunday sale law discussed.

Apr. 3   Eleanor Roosevelt sees no reason not to serve beer at the White House

Apr 4/5   NJ bans beer on Sundays and restricts it on weekdays from 7 AM-midnight. Brewery license fee= $50 and Three cent tax on each gallon sold. Big rush for beer licenses.

Apr 13   Max Hessel and Joseph Greenberg of Reading PA are murdered in the Elizabeth-Carteret Hotel. Hessel was an intimate of Ay Lillien, the NJ Rum King. Apparent mob hit.

Jun 6   William "Bill" Lambert of New Village, NJ charged with assault/battery fined $75. One year prison sentence suspended.

Jun 14   Massachusetts becomes 11th State in favor of Repeal.

Jun 16   NJ Beer Commission recommends beer sales over bars and Sunday beer sales after 1 PM. (Action was approved by NJ Assembly on 19 June by vote 34 to 16)

Jul 17   Four to five million bushels of Rye would find an outlet with passage of Repeal.

Aug 3   Walt Smith conviction for drunken driving is reversed, since doctor's exam came 4 hrs after arrest and two witnesses denied he was intoxicated.

Dec 5   Federal Prohibition Ends